Challenge

Klassen 11 – 13

Englisch für Berufliche Gymnasien
Bundesausgabe/Niedersachsen-Ausgabe

Vocabulary Notebook

von
Oliver Frank

Ernst Klett Verlag
Stuttgart · Leipzig

Challenge Klassen 11–13

Englisch für Berufliche Gymnasien
Bundesausgabe/Niedersachsen-Ausgabe
Vocabulary Notebook

Werkübersicht:

Schülerbuch Bundesausgabe, Klasse 11, 978-3-12-809208-9
Schülerbuch Bundesausgabe, Klassen 12/13, 978-3-12-809209-6
Schülerbuch Niedersachsen, Klassen 11–13, 978-3-12-809217-1
Workbook und EXAM TRAINING mit Audio-CD, Bundesausgabe, Klassen 11-13, 978-3-12-809213-3
Workbook und EXAM TRAINING mit Audio-CD, Niedersachsen, Klassen 11–13, 978-3-12-809219-5
Vocabulary Notebook, Klassen 11–13, 978-3-12-809214-0
Lehrerhandbuch inkl. Digitalem Lehrer-Service, Klassen 11-13, 978-3-12-809212-6
Schülerbuch-Paket Bundesausgabe: Schülerbuch Klasse 11 + Schülerbuch Klassen 12/13, 978-3-12-809215-7
Arbeitsmaterial-Paket Bundesausgabe: Workbook/EXAM TRAINING + Vocabulary Notebook, Klassen 11-13, 978-3-12-809216-4
Arbeitsmaterial-Paket Niedersachsen: Workbook/EXAM TRAINING + Vocabulary Notebook, Klassen 11–13, 978-3-12-809222-5

1. Auflage 1 6 5 4 3 | 2021 20 19 18

Projektleitung: Matthias Rupp, Karin Altrichter
Redaktion: Gaby Bauer-Negenborn, Weßling
Herstellung: Angelika Lindner, Sarah Ganser
Satz und Gestaltung: Ulrike Promies, Metzingen
Umschlaggestaltung: Projektteam des Verlages
Reproduktion: Meyle + Müller Medien-Management, Pforzheim
Druck: Medienhaus Plump GmbH, Rheinbreitbach

Printed in Germany
ISBN 978-3-12-809214-0

9 783128 092140

Vorwort

Das **Vocabulary Notebook** zu **Challenge Bund/Niedersachsen** enthält den thematischen Aufbauwortschatz für Klasse 11 (Topics 1.1 bis 1.5) und die Klassen 12 und 13 (Topics 2.1 bis 2.10) an Beruflichen Gymnasien.

Es werden nicht nur die deutschen Bedeutungen der Wörter geliefert, sondern auch Definitionen und Beispielsätze sowie Synonyme, Antonyme und Hinweise zur Wortfamilie angeboten. Die Vielfalt der Aufgaben verhindert, dass das Erlernen der Vokabeln eintönig wird und hilft Ihnen, sich die Wörter besser einzuprägen.

Damit auch die richtige Aussprache der Wörter geübt werden kann, sind alle Vokabeln vertont. Über den **Challenge-Code** (siehe Übersicht auf S. 121) können Sie sich das **Talking vocabulary** als MP3-Dateien zum Anhören der korrekten Aussprache kostenlos unter www.klett.de herunterladen.

Bei schwierigen Wörtern wurde im **Vocabulary Notebook** die Lautschrift ergänzt. Auf S. 4 finden Sie eine Übersicht über das **Phonetic alphabet** und einen Hinweis zum **Videotraining: Englische Aussprache**. Nutzen Sie die Online-Angebote und Sie werden feststellen, dass sich Ihre Aussprache schon nach kurzer Zeit deutlich verbessert.

Wir wünschen Ihnen viel Erfolg!

Autor und Redaktion

Zum Abschluss noch ein paar wichtige Tipps zum Vokabellernen. Wenn Sie Vokabeln nur kurz vor einem Test oder einer Klassenarbeit wiederholen, werden Sie im Kurzzeitgedächtnis gespeichert. Um Wörter dauerhaft abzuspeichern, ist es hilfreich:

- regelmäßig in kleineren Einheiten zu lernen (15 Minuten am Tag sind besser als einmal in der Woche drei Stunden am Stück),
- nicht mehr als 10–15 Vokabeln auf einmal zu lernen,
- die gelernten Vokabeln aufzuschreiben (z. B. einen Karteikasten anzulegen),
- das Gelernte kurz vor dem Schlafengehen zu wiederholen (Informationen werden so in das Langzeitgedächtnis übernommen und bleiben dort länger präsent),
- die Vokabeln mindestens dreimal zu wiederholen.

Phonetic alphabet • Lautschrift

Perfekte englische Aussprache leicht gemacht: Mit dem Lernprogramm zur englischen Lautschrift können Sie alle Laute einüben. Wählen Sie einfach in der Navigation rechts den entsprechenden Reiter (Vowels oder Consonants) aus und dann klicken Sie auf das gewünschte phonetische Symbol. Sprechen Sie die Wörter laut nach.
Unter www.klett.de geben Sie einfach den Code **n633sn** ein. Von dort aus können Sie die Webanwendung online starten.

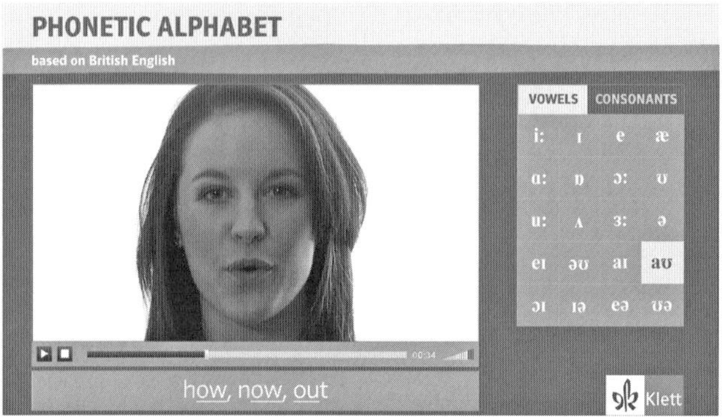

[:] bedeutet, dass der vorangegangene Laut lang ist
[ˈ] bedeutet, dass die folgende Silbe eine Hauptbetonung erhält
[ˌ] bedeutet, dass die folgende Silbe eine Nebenbetonung erhält
[‿] bedeutet, dass die beiden Laute miteinander verbunden werden

[i:] meet [mi:t]
[ɑ:] father [ˈfɑ:ðə]
[ɔ:] morning [ˈmɔ:niŋ]
[u:] blue [blu:]
[ɜ:] German [ˈdʒɜ:mən]

[ɪ] in [ɪn]
[e] yes [yes]
[æ] thanks [θæŋks]
[ʌ] much [mʌtʃ]
[ɒ] what [wɒt]
[ʊ] good [gʊd]
[ə] number [ˈnʌmbə]

[eɪ] name [neɪm]
[aɪ] my [maɪ]
[ɔɪ] boiled [bɔɪld]

[əʊ] phone [fəʊn]
[aʊ] now [naʊ]
[ɪə] hear [hɪə]
[eə] where [weə]
[ʊə] tourist [ˈtʊərɪst]

[p] pop [pɒp]
[b] bye [baɪ]
[t] town [taʊn]
[d] drink [drɪŋk]
[k] coffee [ˈkɒfɪ]
[g] good [gʊd]

[tʃ] church [tʃɜ:tʃ]
[dʒ] job [dʒɒb]
[f] fine [faɪn]
[v] very [ˈverɪ]

[θ] thanks [θæŋks]
[ð] this [ðɪs]
[s] son [sʌn]
[z] is [ɪz]
[ʃ] she [ʃi:]
[ʒ] television [ˌtelɪˈvɪʒn]

[h] he [hi:]
[m] my [maɪ]
[n] now [naʊ]
[ŋ] evening [ˈi:vnɪŋ]
[l] like [ˈlaɪk]
[r] room [ru:m]
[w] we [wi:]
[y] yes [yes]

Inhalt

Abkürzungen und Symbole

BE	britisches Englisch
AE	amerikanisches Englisch
e.g.	Anwendungsbeispiel
=	synonym
↔	opposite
→	word family

Service im Internet

Unter **Challenge Bundesausgabe / Niedersachsen-Ausgabe-Online** finden Sie die Vokabeln des Vocabulary Notebook zum Download im MP3-Format. Einfach auf www.klett.de/online gehen und in das Suchfeld den Challenge-Code eingeben. Weitere Hinweise finden Sie auf Seite 121.

Topic 1.1 Being young today

Topic vocabulary

A Growing up		
interior [ɪn'tɪəriə] minister	Innenminister(in)	↔ foreign minister
recent	neulich	= not long ago
phenomenon [fɪ'nɒmɪnən]	Phänomen	= sth. extraordinary or exceptional
to ban	verbieten	→ a ban
in advance	im Vorfeld	→ to advance (= voranschreiten)
evidence	Beweis	→ evident
duty	Pflicht	e.g. on duty (= im Dienst)
municipal [mju:'nɪsɪpl]	städtisch	e.g. municipal administration
appropriate [ə'prəʊpriət]	angemessen	= suitable
to intervene [ˌɪntə'vi:n]	intervenieren, einschreiten	→ intervention
to detain	in Gewahrsam nehmen	→ detainment
custody ['kʌstədi]	Polizeigewahrsam	e.g. police custody
to extinguish [ɪk'stɪŋgwɪʃ]	löschen	e.g. a fire extinguisher
mayor [meə]	Bürgermeister(in)	= the head of a town or city
authorities [ɔ:'θɒrətiz]	Behörden	e.g. tax authorities
crowd [kraʊd]	(Menschen-)Menge	e.g. There was a big crowd at the scene of the accident.
B Teenagers and technology		
prevalent ['prevələnt]	vorherrschend	= widely accepted
to boast [bəʊst]	angeben	= to show off
to validate	bestätigen	= to confirm
perilous ['perələs]	gefährlich	= dangerous
to blush	erröten	= to flush

predecessor ['pri:dɪˌsesə]	Vorgänger(in)	↔ successor
to reckon	vermuten	= to guess
barely ['beəli]	kaum	= hardly
to gossip ['gɒsɪp]	tratschen, lästern	→ the gossip
to tease sb.	jmdn hänseln	→ a tease (= ein Plagegeist)
to facilitate [fə'sɪlɪteɪt]	erleichtern	→ facilitation (= Erleichterung)
to rage [reɪdʒ]	toben	→ rage (= Rage, Wut)
C Young people and families		
to acquire	erwerben	= to buy
dedicated	engagiert	→ dedication
determined	entschlossen	→ determination
D Binge drinking		
humiliating [hju:'mɪlieɪtɪŋ]	demütigend	= embarrassing
to tackle sth.	etw. angehen	= to fight
maturity [mə'tjʊərəti]	Reife	↔ immaturity
peer pressure	Gruppenzwang	= pressure from people your own age
confidence	Selbstvertrauen	→ confident (= zuversichtlich)
to encourage	ermutigen	↔ to discourage
to decrease	zurückgehen, sinken	↔ to increase
E Young people and the future		
right track	richtiger Weg	e.g. to be on the right track
consumption	Konsum	→ to consume
Exam practice		
juvenile ['dʒu:vənaɪl]	Jugendliche(r)	= youngster
to engage in sth.	sich mit etw. befassen	→ engagement
to sample	etw. ausprobieren	= to try
to opt out ['ɒpt‿aʊt]	aussteigen	e.g. opt-out clause (= Ausstiegsklausel)

Additional vocabulary

Anspruch	entitlement [ɪn'taɪtlmənt]	→ to be entitled (= berechtigt sein)
Aufsatz	essay ['eseɪ]	= a short piece of writing about a particular subject
Ausgesetztsein	exposure [ɪk'spəʊʒə]	→ to expose
Begabung	ability	= talent
die Schule abbrechen	to drop out of school	→ a high school drop out
die Schule schwänzen	to play truant	→ truancy
Druck	pressure	e.g. peer pressure (= Gruppenzwang)
durchsetzen	to enforce	→ enforcement
ehrgeizig	ambitious [æm'bɪʃəs]	→ ambition
Eifersucht	jealousy ['dʒeləsi]	→ jealous
einen Hochschulabschluss machen	to graduate from college	→ graduation
Einrichtung	facility	= rooms or services provided for a particular purpose
Erfolg haben	to succeed	↔ to fail
etw. erreichen	to achieve sth.	→ achievement
etw. zugeben	to admit sth.	↔ to deny sth.
Fettleibigkeit	obesity [əʊ'bi:səti]	→ obese
Geduld	patience ['peɪʃəns]	→ patient
Gewohnheit	habit	→ habitual
Heranwachsende(r)	adolescent [ˌædəl'esənt]	→ adolescence [ˌædəl'esəns] (= Pubertät)
Internat	boarding school	↔ day school
jmdn erfüllen	to fulfil sb.	e.g. a fulfilling job
Jugendkultur	youth culture	→ youth crime
Karriere, Beruf	career	e.g. a career woman
Klischee	stereotype ['steriəʊtaɪp]	= a very firm and simple idea of sth.
Lebensstil	lifestyle	= way of life

Marke	label	= brand
Mobbing	bullying ['bʊliɪŋ]	→ to bully
Note	mark (BE)	= grade (AE)
oberflächlich	superficial [ˌsu:pə'fɪʃəl]	↔ profound, deep
Scheitern, Versagen	failure ['feɪljə]	→ to fail
Schulleiter	headmaster (BE)	= principal (AE)
Selbstverständnis	self-image	= self-concept
Selbstwertgefühl	self-esteem	e.g. low self-esteem
sich auf jmdn verlassen	to rely on sb.	= to trust sb.
sich einleben	to settle into	→ settlement (= Begleichung, Ansiedelung)
sich streiten	to quarrel ['kwɒrəl]	= to argue, to fight
sich wieder verheiraten	to remarry	= to marry again
Stress	stress	→ stressful, to be stressed out
verwundbar	vulnerable ['vʌlnərəbl]	= can be hurt easily
weiterführende Schule	secondary school	= high school (US)

Exercises

a) Word family: Fill in the missing words in the table (no -ing or -ed forms). Use a dictionary and translate them into German.

Noun	Verb	Adjective
	– to validate – bestätigen	
	– – –	– vulnerable –
	– to acquire –	– – –
	– to succeed –	
	– to rely on sb. –	

b) Complete the text with the verbs from below.

allow | are doing | wanders | create | interact | describes | give | is | can be | can design | take | organise | keep | may seem | provide | offer | provides

A second life at Second Life

The computer screen and the internet ________________ (1) opportunities for quick communication and seemingly endless information. And now they can also ________________ (2) you what many so ________________ (3) to want: a second life. Well, a virtual second life, but a pretty realistic one.

Sites like Habbo and Second Life ________________ (4) platforms from which subscribers can build up their own virtual worlds, and more and more people ________________ (5) it. But what is it exactly that these virtual worlds ________________ (6)?

____________ (7) Habbo, for instance. This is a free virtual community for teenagers where you ________________________ (8) your own personal room, ____________ (9) your own pet, ________________ (10) parties and meet new people. It also ________________ (11) numerous games and contests to take part in.

Second Life ____________ (12) the equivalent for adults with already over four million users. It ________________ (13) itself as a "3D online digital world imagined, created and owned by its residents". New members are invited to create an avatar, or a virtual person, who ________________ (14) as strange as their ideas and imagination ________________ (15). This person then ________________ (16) through the three-dimensional landscapes and can chat and ________________ (17) with other avatars on the site.

From: *Read On*, 4/2007, www.sprachzeitungen.de

c) Find the words in this topic that match these definitions.

1. to become familiar with sth.: ______________________
2. to officially forbid: ______________________
3. to step in in order to prevent sth.: ______________________
4. to turn red because of embarrassment: ______________________
5. being affected by sth.: ______________________
6. to obtain a degree from college: ______________________
7. spending all your time and effort on sth.: ______________________
8. young person developing into an adult: ______________________
9. fact that supports a belief: ______________________
10. an obligation to do sth.: ______________________
11. your right to have sth.: ______________________
12. to talk about a person, often in a negative way: ______________________
13. to make sth. easier: ______________________
14. to try to make sb. feel embarrassed or annoyed, just for fun:

____

d) Translate the clues below and then write the answers in the grid.

1. oberflächlich
2. erwerben
3. Selbstwertgefühl
4. zugeben
5. veröffentlichen
6. das Schulschwänzen
7. erreichen
8. Fettleibigkeit
9. Geduld

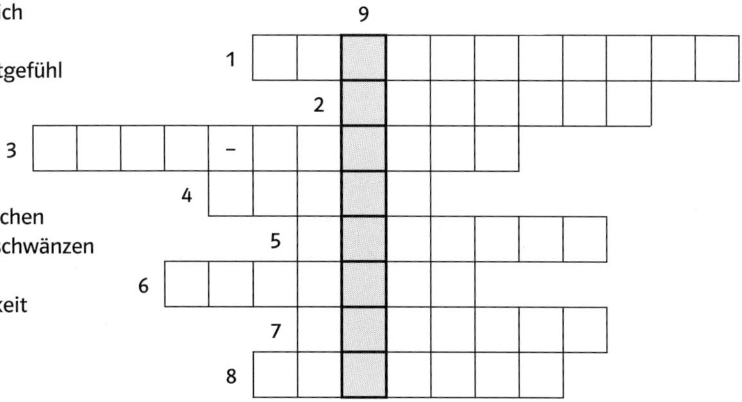

Topic 1.2 Personal identities and social relationships

Topic vocabulary

Getting started		
mother-in-law	Schwiegermutter	→ father-in-law, sister-in-law
to label	beschriften	→ a label
acquaintance [ə'kweɪntəns]	Bekannte(r)	→ to be acquainted with sb. (= mit jmdm bekannt sein)
A Friends		
depth [depθ]	Tiefe	e.g. The pool has a depth of two metres.
intimacy ['ɪntɪməsi]	Intimität	→ intimate
affection	Zuneigung	→ to be affected
mate	Kumpel, Freund(in)	= friend
to accumulate [ə'kju:mjəleɪt]	anhäufen, (sich) ansammeln	= to collect
to abandon	verlassen	= to leave sb. forever
affair	Affäre, Verhältnis	= relationship
to track	verfolgen	= to follow closely
to reveal	bekanntgeben	= to inform public
face value	Nennwert	= the value which is shown on sth.
to exhaust [ɪg'zɔ:st]	ausbeuten, erschöpfen	e.g. She was exhausted by running up the hill.
self-worth	Selbstwert	= the value you give to yourself
self-respect	Selbstachtung	→ self-esteem (= Selbstwertgefühl)
to appreciate sth. [ə'pri:ʃieɪt]	etw. schätzen	→ appreciation (= Anerkennung, Schätzung)
to humiliate [hju:'mɪliəɪt]	demütigen	→ humiliation (= Demütigung)

burden ['bɜ:dən]	Last	e.g. a heavy burden
peer [pɪə]	Gleichaltrige(r)	e.g. peer group (= Alterskohorte)
B Family issues		
guess	Vermutung	→ to guess
coincidence [kəʊ'ɪnsɪdəns]	Zufall	= by accident
unfortunate	bedauernswert	↔ fortunate (= glücklich, günstig)
C Gender stereotypes		
gender ['dʒendə]	Geschlecht	e.g. gender-neutral (= geschlechtsneutral)
stereotype	Stereotyp, Klischee	= a fixed idea what certain people are like
prejudice ['predʒədɪs]	Vorurteil	→ to be prejudiced (= voreingenommen sein)
balance	Rest, Saldo, Gleichgewicht	→ to balance (= etw. ausgleichen, ausbalancieren)
participation	Beteiligung	→ to participate
temporary ['tempərəri]	vorübergehend	↔ permanent
distribution	Verteilung	↔ redistribution (= Umverteilung)
contest	Wettbewerb	→ to contest (= etw. bestreiten, anfechten)
D Volunteering		
billion	Milliarde	= one thousand million
to estimate ['estɪmeɪt]	schätzen	→ estimation
inconvenience [ˌɪnkən'vi:nɪəns]	Unannehmlichkeit	↔ convenience
benefit	Vorteil	= advantage
compassion [kəm'pæʃn]	Mitgefühl	→ compassionate (= mitfühlend)
urgency ['ɜ:dʒənsi]	Dringlichkeit	e.g. utmost urgency (= größte Dringlichkeit)

E Generation Me?		
self-absorbed [ˌselfəb'zɔ:bd]	mit sich selbst beschäftigt	= self-centred
to release	hier: veröffentlichen	e.g. to release a CD
empathy ['empəθi]	Empathie, Mitgefühl	= ability to understand other people's feelings
to label	beschriften, nennen	= to name
to devalue	abwerten	→ devaluation
gender ['dʒendə]	Geschlecht	e.g. gender-neutral
appropriate [ə'prəʊpriət]	angemessen, passend	= suitable
ease	Erleichterung, Bequemlichkeit	= without difficulty
Exam practice		
to decline	sinken, zurückgehen	↔ to rise
to stigmatise ['stɪgmətaɪz]	brandmarken	→ stigma
significance [sɪg'nɪfɪkəns]	Bedeutung	→ significant
impact	Auswirkung	= effect
to bully ['bʊli]	mobben	= to pick on so.
to embed	einbinden	e.g. embedded (= tief verwurzelt)
association [əˌsəʊʃi'eɪʃn]	Verbindung	= connection
to match	übereinstimmen	= to agree with
shift	Veränderung	= change
abuse [ə'bju:s]	Missbrauch	= misuse
to improve	verbessern	→ improvement

Additional vocabulary

Adoption	adoption [ə'dɒpʃən]	→ to put a child up for adoption (= ein Kind zur Adoption freigeben)
Arbeit im Haushalt, lästige Pflicht	chore	= duty

Beherrschung	temper ['tempə]	e.g. to lose one's temper
Berufserfahrung	work experience	e.g. to gain work experience
die Scheidung einreichen	to file for divorce	→ to end in divorce
Eheproblem	marital ['mærɪtəl] problem	→ marital status (= Familienstand)
Eifersucht	jealousy ['dʒeləsi]	→ jealous
ein Jahr aussetzen	to take a gap year	= to take a year off
entmutigend	daunting ['dɔ:ntɪŋ]	↔ encouraging
etw. in Frage stellen	to question sth.	↔ to accept sth.
für jmdn schwärmen	to have a crush on sb. (informal)	= to fancy sb.
gegen jmdn/etw. rebellieren	to rebel [rɪ'bel] against sb./ sth.	→ rebel (= der/die Rebell/in)
gegenseitig	mutual ['mju:tʃuəl]	→ mutuality (= Gegenseitigkeit)
Geschwister	sibling ['sɪblɪŋ]	e.g. sibling rivalry ['raɪvəlri] (= Rivalität unter Geschwistern)
heiraten	to marry	→ to remarry
jmdn kritisieren	to criticize sb. ['krɪtɪsaɪz]	→ criticism
Jugendalter	adolescence [ˌædəl'esəns]	→ adolescent (= Jugendliche/r)
mit jmdm (aus)gehen	to go out with sb. (BE)	→ to date sb. (AE)
Pflegekind	foster child ['fɒstə ˌtʃaɪld]	→ to foster a child (= ein Kind in Pflege nehmen)
Pubertät	puberty ['pju:bəti]	e.g. the onset of puberty
Scheidung	divorce	↔ marriage (= Ehe)
sich trennen	to separate	→ separation (= Trennung)
sich trennen	to split up	= to break up, to call it a day (informal)
so gut wie jmd sein	to live up to sb.	e.g. to live up to sb.'s expectations (= jmds Erwartungen gerecht werden)
Stiefbruder, Stiefschwester	stepbrother, stepsister	→ half-brother, half-sister
Stimmung	mood	e.g. mood swing (= Stimmungsschwankung)

Strauß	bouquet	e.g a bridal bouquet (= Brautstrauß)
streiten	to row [raʊ]	→ to have a row (= sich streiten)
Vormundschaft	custody ['kʌstədi]	e.g. to get custody of a child
zeitgenössisch	contemporary [kən'tempərəri]	e.g. contemporary issue (= aktuelles Problem)
Zeit verbringen, herumlungern	to hang out (informal)	→ hung, hung

Exercises

a) Word family: Fill in the missing words in the table (no -ing or -ed forms). Use a dictionary and translate them into German.

Noun	Verb	Adjective
– depth – Tiefe		
	– to accumulate –	
	– to exhaust –	
– abuse –		
– ease –		

b) Find the words in this topic that match these definitions or synonyms.

1. a very positive feeling: ____________________
2. to make better: ____________________
3. an unfair opinion about sb., formed without enough knowledge: ____________________
4. sb. you have met but do not know too well: ____________________
5. sb. who advises people: ____________________
6. to argue with sb.: ____________________

7. to resist authority: ____________________

8. sex: ____________________

9. importance: ____________________

10. to decrease: ____________________

c) Which of the following words can be combined with which of the expressions in the table? Translate the combined terms into German.

sibling | to foster | behavioral | to lose | peer

bridal | to file for | contemporary | marital | household

	chore	Hausarbeit
	bouquet	
	a child	
	one's temper	
	rivalry	
	divorce	
	art	
	problem	
	pattern	
	group	

d) Find the word or expression in each row which does not go with the others and cross it out. Explain your choice.

1.	☐ mate	☐ friend	☐ peer
2.	☐ to release	☐ to accumulate	☐ to collect
3.	☐ to row	☐ to label	☐ to name
4.	☐ appropriate	☐ unfortunate	☐ suitable
5.	☐ impact	☐ effect	☐ improvement
6.	☐ to track	☐ to follow closely	☐ to reveal

e) **Translate the clues below and then write the answers in the grid.**

Across
1. beschriften
4. Mitgefühl
6. schätzen
8. Pubertät
10. Vorurteil
11. Zuneigung
12. Verteilung
14. Zufall
15. Last
16. Veränderung

Down
2. Missbrauch
3. Bedeutung
5. mobben
7. vorübergehend
9. Stimmung
13. Tiefe

Topic 1.3 Progress and sustainability

Topic vocabulary

Getting started		
renewable [rɪ'nju:əbl] energy	erneuerbare Energie	e.g. solar, wind, hydroelectric
hazardous ['hæzədəs]	gefährlich	= dangerous
A Climate change		
carbon dioxide [ˌkɑ:bndaɪ'ɒksaɪd]	Kohlendioxyd	= a colourless gas that is blamed to cause global warming
vapour ['veɪpə]	Dampf	= steam
to emit	ausstoßen	→ emission
fossil fuel	fossiler Brennstoff	e.g. coal, oil and natural gas are fossil fuels
issue ['ɪʃu:]	Thema	= topic
human-induced [ˌhju:mənɪn'dju:st]	von Menschen erzeugt	= caused by mankind
glacier ['glæsɪə]	Gletscher	= a large amount of ice that moves slowly down a valley
unprecedented [ʌn'presɪdentɪd]	noch nie dagewesen	= never happened before
habitat	Lebensraum	e.g. natural habitat
drought	Dürre	= a long period without rainfall
scarce [skeəs]	knapp	→ scarcity
arid	dürr	= very dry
biodiversity [ˌbaɪəʊdaɪ'vɜ:sətɪ]	Artenvielfalt	= the range of varieties of plants and animals in a particular environment

B Alternative energy		
ambitious [æm'bɪʃəs]	ehrgeizig	→ ambition (= Ehrgeiz, Bestreben)
emission [ɪ'mɪʃən]	Ausstoß, Emission	→ to emit
to require	benötigen	→ requirement (= Anforde-rung, Voraussetzung)
binding ['baɪndɪŋ]	bindend	= mandatory
scale [skeɪl]	Umfang	= extent
to exceed [ɪk'si:d]	übertreffen	= to surpass
demand	Nachfrage	e.g. demand and supply
fossil-fuelled ['fɒsəlˌfju:əld]	fossil angetrieben	= powered by fossil fuels
abundant [ə'bʌndənt]	reichlich	→ abundance (= Überfluss)
natural resource	Bodenschatz	e.g. coal, oil etc.
grid [grɪd]	Netz, Gitter	e.g. electricity grid
overhaul ['əʊvəhɔ:l]	Überarbeitung	→ to overhaul
combustion [kəm'bʌstʃən]	Verbrennung	e.g. combustion engine
to take sth. for granted	etw. als selbstverständlich hinnehmen	→ to grant (= etw. gewähren)
to melt	schmelzen	↔ to freeze
C Saving the planet		
to abuse [ə'bju:z]	missbrauchen	→ the abuse
ancient ['eɪnʃənt]	antik	= very old
enemy	Feind(in)	= foe
D GM and designer food		
attempt [ə'tempt]	Versuch	= effort
vice versa [ˌvaɪsi'vɜ:sə]	umgekehrt	= the other way around
to oppose	bekämpfen, ablehnen	→ opposition (= Widerstand, Opposition)
beverage ['bevərɪdʒ]	Getränk	= drink
ingredient [ɪn'gri:diənt]	Zutat	= a component part of sth.

texture ['tekstʃə]	Konsistenz	= the way sth. feels
concern	Sorge	= worry
to admit	zugeben	= to confess
to replicate [replɪ'keɪt]	nachmachen	→ replication (= Kopie)
E Eco-tourism		
to compile [kəm'paɪl]	zusammenstellen, zusammentragen	→ compilation (= Sammlung)
outstanding	herausragend	= excellent
to demand	verlangen, einfordern	→ the demand
to assess [ə'ses]	beurteilen, einschätzen	→ assessment
host	Gastgeber	e.g. host family
unique [ju:'ni:k]	einzigartig	→ uniqueness
to appeal to	ansprechen, attraktiv sein für	= to attract sb.
to harm	schädigen, schaden	= to damage
occasionally [ə'keɪʒənəli]	gelegentlich	= sometimes
sensible	vernünftig	↔ sensitive (= sensibel)
to pollute	verschmutzen	→ pollution
cruise [kru:z]	Kreuzfahrt	= a pleasure trip on a luxury ship
to claim	behaupten	→ a claim (= Forderung, Behauptung)
evidence ['evɪdəns]	Nachweis, Beweis	→ evident (= offensichtlich)
commitment [kə'mɪtmənt]	Engagement, Einsatz	→ to be committed
environment	Umwelt	→ environmental
to cater for	sorgen für	→ catering
Exam practice		
inconvenient [ˌɪnkən'vi:niənt]	ungünstig	↔ convenient
to subsidise ['sʌbsɪdaɪz]	subventionieren	→ subsidy (= Subvention)
to slaughter ['slɔ:tə]	schlachten	= to kill

excessive [ɪk'sesɪv]	übermäßig	= over the top
deliberate [dɪ'lɪbərət]	absichtlich	= on purpose

Additional vocabulary

Abwasser	sewage ['suːɪdʒ]	= effluent, waste water
Atem-	respiratory [rɪ'spɪrətərɪ]	= connected with breathing
ausgestorben	extinct	→ extinction
Dünger	fertilizer ['fɜːtɪlaɪzə]	e.g. artificial fertilizer
Energie sparen	to conserve energy	= to save energy
Ernte, Feldfrucht	crop	e.g. wheat and rice
Ertrag	yield [jiːld]	= the amount of crops or profits that you get
FCKWs	CFCs	e.g. CFCs can destroy the ozone layer.
etw. freisetzen	to release sth.	e.g. Heat trapping gases are released into the atmosphere.
geothermisch	geothermal [ˌdʒiːə'θɜːməl]	e.g. geothermal heat
Gerät	appliance [ə'plaɪəns]	e.g. household appliances
den Gezeiten unterworfen	tidal	→ tide
häuslich	domestic	e.g. for domestic use
Hautkrebs	skin cancer	e.g. Solar radiation can cause skin cancer.
Hitzewelle	heatwave	= a period of very hot weather
Katastrophe	disaster	= catastrophe [kə'tæstrəfɪ]
Klimaveränderung	climate change	e.g. Climate change is caused by the greenhouse effect.
Mangel	shortage	= lack, shortfall
Meeresspiegel	sea level	e.g. 200 m above sea level
Reinigungsmittel	detergent [dɪ'tɜːdʒənt]	e.g. biodegradable detergent
nicht mehr rückgängig zu machen	irreversible [ˌɪrɪ'vɜːsəbl]	↔ reversible

rücksichtslos	reckless ['rekləs]	= irresponsible
Schadstoff	pollutant	→ to pollute, pollution
schädlich	harmful	↔ harmless
Schädlingsbekämpfungs-mittel	pesticide ['pestɪsaɪd]	↔ herbicide (Unkraut-vernichtungsmittel)
Selbstwertgefühl	self-esteem [ˌselfɪ'sti:m]	= respect for oneself
städtisch	urban	↔ rural
Veranstaltungsort	venue ['venju:]	= place organised events take place
sich verringern, sich vermindern	to deplete	→ depletion
verschmutzen, vergiften	to contaminate	= to poison
Wasserkraft	hydroelectric [ˌhaɪdrəʊɪ'lektrɪk] energy	→ hydroelectric power plant
Zugang	access	e.g. restricted access

Exercises

a) Find the words in this topic that match these definitions. Then find the German meaning.

Definition	English	German
1. to support financially		
2. to copy		
3. not to question sth.		
4. a long period without rainfall		
5. respect for oneself		
6. the place where an organised event takes place		
7. to be against		

Definition	English	German
8. to reduce the amount of sth.		
9. the regular rising and lowering of the sea		
10. a substance that makes air, water, or soil dirty		
11. more than enough		
12. materials or substances occurring in nature which can be exploited for economic gain		
13. revision		
14. the process of burning sth.		
15. irresponsible		

b) What's the word in English?

1. gefährlich: ____________________
2. Dürre: ____________________
3. Lebensraum: ____________________
4. Netz: ____________________
5. antik: ____________________
6. bindend: ____________________
7. Umfang: ____________________
8. Gletscher: ____________________
9. Dampf: ____________________
10. Ertrag: ____________________
11. absichtlich: ____________________
12. Beweis: ____________________

c) Complete the word web with words or phrases from below.

coal | pollution | cheap | no CO_2-emissions (2x) | geothermal | dangerous | fossil | depleting | comparably cheap | nuclear | hydroelectric | natural gas | non-depleting | renewable | still expensive | CO_2-emissions | wind | tidal

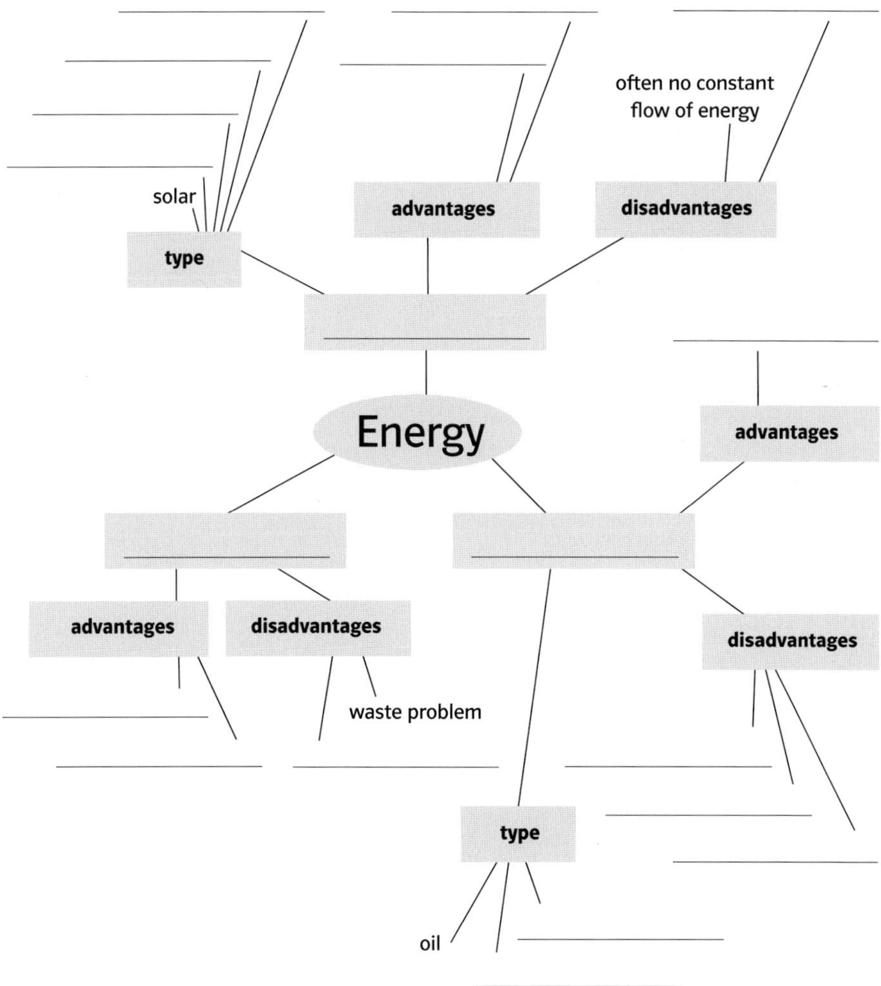

d) Complete the text with the verbs from below. Two verbs don't fit!

affect	affects	are	do not have	face
haven't	is (2x)	is made worse	is needed	
will leave	will suffer	will experience	is often polluted	

A way out of world water crisis?

A worldwide water crisis ____________ (1) likely to get worse over the next 25 years with billions of people affected by a global crisis. Already about 450 million people in 29 countries ____________ (2) serious water shortages which ____________ (3) the wealthiest and poorest nations. Expanding economies and populations ____________ (4) competing for fewer sources of fresh water.

According to Frank Richman, the director of the International Water Management Institute, the demand for water ____________ (5) some of the world's major rivers dry throughout most of the year. "Urban centres ____________ (6) water shortages. But the rural poor ____________ (7) the most serious consequences. Many people already ____________ (8) access to drinking water and to the quantity and quality of water that ____________ (9) to grow food." The crisis ____________ (10) because the freshwater ____________ (11) by industrial waste and by increasing amounts of raw sewage. This ____________ (12) the main cause of diseases in some countries.

Topic 1.4 Britain and the United States

Topic vocabulary

A Britain and the US: A special relationship		
to found	gründen	→ foundation
persecution [ˌpɜːsɪˈkjuːʃn]	Verfolgung	→ to persecute
declaration	Erklärung	→ to declare
famine [ˈfæmɪn]	Hungersnot	e.g. famine wages (= Hungerlohn)
harvest [ˈhɑːvɪst]	Ernte	→ to harvest
to emigrate	auswandern	↔ to immigrate
reluctantly [rɪˈlʌktəntlɪ]	zögerlich	→ reluctance (= Zögern)
B Welcome to America		
approximately	ungefähr	= about
resource	Vorrat, Rohstoff	e.g. renewable resource (= erneuerbarer Rohstoff)
desertification [dɪˌzɜːtɪfɪˈkeɪʃn]	Versteppung	→ desert
estimate	Schätzung	→ to estimate
C City or suburb?		
rural [ˈrʊərəl]	ländlich	↔ urban (= städtisch)
to preserve	bewahren	→ preservation
condominium [ˌkɒndəˈmɪnɪəm]	Eigentumswohnung	→ condo [ˈkɒndəʊ] (short for condominium)
to predict	vorhersagen	= to tell in advance
vacant [ˈveɪkənt]	leer stehend, frei	→ vacancy
lot	Grundstück	= building ground
obesity [əˈbiːsɪtɪ]	Fettleibigkeit	→ obese

scarce [skeəs]	knapp	→ scarcity
crucial ['kru:ʃl]	sehr wichtig	= essential
to endanger	gefährden	e.g. endangered species
to interfere [ˌɪntə'fɪə]	sich einmischen	→ interference
D 9/11		
initial [ɪ'nɪʃl]	erste(r,s)	= first
to hijack ['haɪdʒæk]	entführen	→ hijacker
magnitude ['mægnɪtju:d]	Größe, Ausmaß	= extent
to witness	mit ansehen, bezeugen	→ the witness
to respond	antworten, reagieren	= to answer, to react
janitor (AE) ['dʒænɪtə]	Hausmeister	= caretaker
executive [ɪg'zekjətɪv]	Führungskraft	e.g. CEO – Chief Executive Officer (≈ Vorstandsvorsitzende/r)
to gather ['gæðə]	zusammenkommen	= to get together
donation	Spende	→ to donate, donor
volunteer [ˌvɒlən'tɪə]	Freiwillige(r)	e.g. volunteer organisation
to affect	beeinflussen	→ the effect
sacrifice ['sækrɪfaɪs]	Opfer	→ to sacrifice
previous ['pri:vɪəs]	vorherig	= prior
tremendous [trə'mendəs]	enorm, gewaltig	= enormous
concrete ['kɒŋkri:t]	Beton	e.g. concrete building
descent [dɪ'sent]	Abstieg	→ to descend
to encounter	antreffen	= to meet
debris ['debri:]	Schutt, Unrat	e.g. a pile of debris (= Schutthaufen)
pigeon ['pɪdʒɪn]	Taube	= bird you often see in cities

E Talking about Britain		
population [ˌpɒpjəˈleɪʃn]	Bevölkerung	e.g. population density
mountain range	Bergkette	= a group of mountains
densely	dicht	→ density
F A journey around Great Britain		
discomfort	Unannehmlichkeit	= inconvenience
itinerary [aɪˈtɪnərəri]	Reiseroute, Reiseplan	e.g. travel itinerary
crucial [ˈkru:ʃəl]	entscheidend	= decisive
Exam practice		
conclusion [kənˈklu:ʒn]	Schlussfolgerung	e.g. to draw a conclusion
to take for granted	als gegeben hinnehmen	→ to grant (= etw. gewähren)

Additional vocabulary

Armut	poverty	↔ wealth
Einkaufszentrum	shopping centre (BE)	= shopping mall (AE)
Obdachlosigkeit	homelessness	→ a homeless person
öffentliches Verkehrsmittel	public transport	e.g. underground system
pendeln	to commute [kəˈmju:t]	→ commuter
sanitäre Anlagen	sanitation [sæniˈteɪʃn]	e.g. poor sanitation
souverän (Staat), hoheitlich regiert	sovereign [ˈsɒvərɪn]	→ sovereignty [ˈsɒvrənti] (= Eigenständigkeit eines Staates)
am Stadtrand	on the outskirts	↔ city centre
Stadtverwaltung	municipal council [mju:ˈnɪsɪpl ˌkaʊnsl]	= city council
Stau	congestion [kənˈdʒestʃn]	→ to be congested
etw. umgeben	to surround sth.	→ surroundings
Umweltverschmutzung	pollution [pʊˈlu:ʃn]	→ to pollute

Unterkunft	accommodation [əˌkɒməˈdeɪʃn]	→ to accommodate sb. (= jmdn unterbringen)
Wohnviertel	residential area	↔ business area
Zwangsräumung	eviction [ɪˈvɪkʃn]	→ to evict sb.

Exercises

a) Find the words in this topic that match these definitions.

1. process in which fertile land dries up: ____________________
2. to keep in the original state: ____________________
3. treating sb. badly, especially because of their religious or political beliefs: ____________________
4. very dry (climate): ____________________
5. all the people living in a particular place or area: ____________________
6. sb. who travels a long distance to work every day: ____________________
7. a period of starvation: ____________________
8. to need sth.: ____________________
9. to kidnap a plane or other vehicle: ____________________

b) Translate the clues below and write the answers in the grid.

1. trocken, dürr
2. Freiwillige(r)
3. Armut
4. leer, frei stehend
5. Umweltverschmutzung
6. ländlich

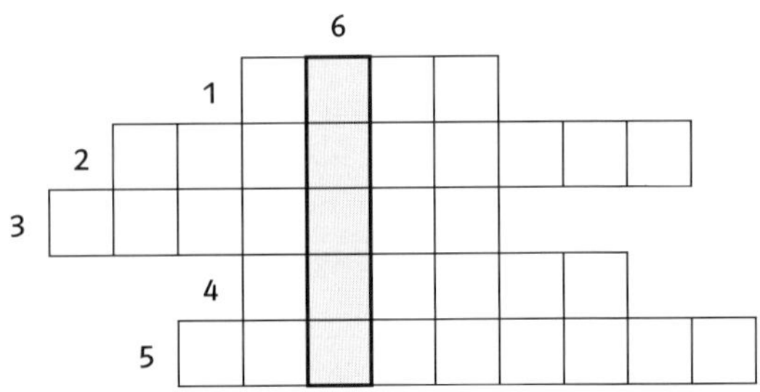

c) Complete the text with the verbs from below.

say | printed | write | be avoided | must call | is made up | think | does not include | has | refer to | mean (2x) | is (3x) | want | can be | call | says | are

The UK, England and Britain

A good quiz question: What do you ________________ (1) the European country that ________________ (2) GB on its cars? Too easy? You ________________ (3) it is England? Well, you ________________ (4) wrong. The title of the country ________________ (5) on the passport is: the United Kingdom of Great Britain and Northern Ireland. That is the official name which ________________ (6) shortened to the UK.

On its website, the British Government ________________ (7):

"The UK ______________________ (8) of England, Scotland, Wales and Northern Ireland. Great Britain (or just Britain) ______________________ (9) Northern Ireland."

In fact, many still say and __________ (10) 'Britain' when they ________________ (11) the UK. However, Great Britain should definitely ________________ (12). And you should never ________________ (13) or write England when you ________________ (14) the UK. England ________________ (15) only a part of the UK, and a Scot, Northern Irish or Welsh person might be very insulted if you ________________ (16) them as English.

There ________________ (17) no adjective from UK, so if you ________________ (18) to talk about people from the UK you ______________________ (19) them British. A person from the UK ______________________ (20) a Briton or a UK resident.

From: *Read On*, 5/2007, www.sprachzeitungen.de

d) Word family: Fill in the missing words in the table (no -ing or -ed forms). Use a dictionary and translate them into German.

Noun	Verb	Adjective
	– to predict – vorhersagen	
		– responsive –
– volunteer –		
– population –		

e) Find the word or expression in each row which does not go with the others. Explain your choice.

1.	☐ impact	☐ effect	☐ extent
2.	☐ sovereignty	☐ crucial	☐ essential
3.	☐ to meet	☐ to commute	☐ to encounter
4.	☐ debris	☐ prior	☐ previous
5.	☐ completely	☐ doubtful	☐ entirely
6.	☐ initial	☐ rural	☐ first
7.	☐ vacant	☐ approximately	☐ about

f) What's the word in English?

1. Lebensraum: ______________________
2. Ernte: ______________________
3. Schädlingsbekämpfungsmittel: ______________________
4. Spende: ______________________
5. Zwangsräumung: ______________________
6. Beton: ______________________

Topic 1.5 Private and professional communication

Topic vocabulary

Getting started		
substitute ['sʌbstɪtjuːt]	Ersatz	= replacement
elaborate [ɪ'læbərət]	kompliziert	= complicated
to found	gründen	→ foundation
A Communicating online		
obsessed	besessen	e.g. Tom was obsessed with football.
selfish	egoistisch	= egoistic
to establish	aufbauen	→ establishment
to maintain [meɪn'teɪn]	aufrechterhalten	→ maintenance (= Instandhaltung)
spouse [spaʊs]	Ehegatte/-gattin	= husband or wife
B Letter writing – a lost art?		
to commission	in Auftrag geben	e.g. to commission a survey
to convey [kən'veɪ]	vermitteln	= to get across
punctuation	Interpunktion	e.g. colons, question marks etc.
literate ['lɪtərət]	lese- und schreibkundig	↔ illiterate
literacy ['lɪtərəsi]	Lese- und Schreibfähigkeit	↔ illiteracy
sponsorship	Förderung	→ to sponsor
to enhance	verbessern	= to improve
C Communicating at work		
majority [mə'dʒɒrəti]	Mehrzahl, Mehrheit	→ major
privacy	Privatsphäre	→ private
to remain	bleiben	e.g. Please remain seated.

progress	Fortschritt	= improvement or development
destination	Ziel	e.g. a holiday destination
intended	hier: bestimmt	→ to intend (= beabsichtigen)
enquiry [ɪnˈkwaɪəri]	Anfrage	e.g. a telephone enquiry
offer	Angebot	e.g. I accepted the offer.
order	Bestellung, Auftrag	→ to order
brochure [ˈbrəʊʃə]	Prospekt, Broschüre	↔ prospect (= Aussicht)
delivery	Lieferung	e.g. delivery times (= Lieferzeiten)
quotation	hier: Angebot, Kostenvoranschlag	= offer
to proceed	fortfahren	= to continue sth.
invoice [ˈɪnvɔɪs]	Rechnung	→ to invoice (= in Rechnung stellen)
discount	Rabatt, Nachlass	→ to discount (= etw. abziehen)
D Office life		
package	Gehalt plus Bonuszahlungen	e.g. The advertised position offers a good package.
track record	Erfolgsgeschichte	e.g. We are looking for a manager with a proven track record.
to debrief [ˌdiːˈbriːf]	einen Einsatzbericht geben	= to give feedback
sick leave	Fehlzeit durch Krankheit	= time off work granted due to illness
subtly [ˈsʌtli]	fast unmerklich	= in a way that is hardly noticeable
impoverished [ɪmˈpɒvərɪʃt]	verarmt	= poorer than before
Exam practice		
to expose	aussetzen (einer Gefahr, einem Risiko)	→ exposure
to hinder	behindern	= to limit

habit	Gewohnheit	→ habitual (= gewöhnlich)
appropriate [ə'prəʊpriət]	passend	= suitable, fitting
to feature ['fi:tʃə]	etw. als Besonderheit ausweisen	→ feature (= besonderes Kennzeichen)

Additional vocabulary

ab Lager	ex stock	e.g. Can the goods be delivered ex stock?
aktuell	latest	↔ actual (= tatsächlich)
Angebotspalette	range	e.g. range of products
Auftauchen	emergence [ɪ'mɜ:dʒəns]	→ to emerge
Außendienstmitarbeiter(in)	representative [ˌreprɪ'zentətɪv]	e.g. a sales representative
Ausstellung	exhibition	→ to exhibit (= ausstellen)
Banküberweisung	bank transfer	= remittance
Bedingungen	terms	e.g. terms of payment and delivery
bestätigen	to acknowledge [ək'nɒlɪdʒ]	→ acknowledgement
dankbar sein	to be grateful	= to be thankful
Dienstleistung	service	e.g. unsatisfactory service
Einführungsrabatt	introductory discount	→ to introduce (= einführen)
einschließen, mit sich bringen	to involve	→ involvement
empfehlen	to recommend	→ recommendation
Erhalt	receipt [rɪ'si:t]	→ to receive
Fehler	flaw [flɔ:]	→ flawless (= fehlerfrei)
gewähren	to grant	e.g. to grant a discount
hochwertig	high-end	= high quality
Lager	warehouse	↔ department store (= Warenhaus)
laut, gemäß	according to	→ in accordance with (= in Übereinstimmung mit)
Lieferung	consignment [kən'saɪnmənt]	= delivery

Mehrwertsteuer	VAT [ˌviːeɪ'tiː]	= value added tax
Mengenrabatt	quantity discount	= volume discount
Messe	fair	e.g. trade fair (= Handelsmesse)
Muster, Probe(exemplar)	sample	→ to sample (= etw. proben, kosten)
platzieren, erteilen	to place	e.g. to place an order
schätzen, begrüßen	to appreciate [ə'priːʃieɪt]	→ appreciation (= Wertschätzung, Anerkennung)
sich beziehen auf	to refer to	→ in reference to (= in Bezug auf)
Skonto	cash discount	e.g. For payment within 10 days we grant 2.5 % cash discount.
umfangreich	substantial [səb'stænʃəl]	e.g. a substantial order
unverbindlich	without obligation	= not binding
versenden	to dispatch	= to send

Exercises

a) **Word family: Fill in the missing words in the table (no -ing or -ed forms). Use a dictionary and translate them into German.**

Noun	Verb	Adjective
– substitute – Ersatz		
		– elaborate –
		– obsessed, obsessive –
	– to intend –	– – –
– progress –		

b) Find the words in this topic that match these definitions or synonyms.

1. to be able to read and write: ______________________
2. to stay: ______________________
3. to establish or to set up: ______________________
4. to think only about oneself: ______________________
5. a bill: ______________________
6. opposite of minority: ______________________
7. to make sth. better: ______________________
8. to welcome sth.: ______________________
9. to confirm sth.: ______________________
10. a mistake: ______________________
11. to come up: ______________________
12. a room or building for the storage of merchandise or commodities:

____

c) Find the word or expression in each row which does not go with the others. Explain your choice.

1.	☐ to enhance	☐ to improve	☐ to found
2.	☐ to proceed	☐ to intend	☐ to continue
3.	☐ to get across	☐ to maintain	☐ to convey
4.	☐ substantial	☐ elaborate	☐ complicated
5.	☐ prospect	☐ prospectus	☐ brochure
6.	☐ consignment	☐ delivery	☐ enquiry
7.	☐ progress	☐ improvement	☐ intention
8.	☐ latest	☐ actual	☐ current
9.	☐ selfish	☐ complicated	☐ egoistic
10.	☐ order	☐ quotation	☐ offer

d) Translate the clues below and then write the answers in the grid.

Across
3. Ersatz
5. laut
8. Mehrwertsteuer
9. Muster
12. Auftauchen
13. empfehlen
15. umfangreich

Down
1. Rabatt
2. Ehegatte/-gattin
4. Bedingungen
6. einschließen
7. Messe
10. Nachfrage
11. Banküberweisung
14. Angebotspalette
16. Angebot

Topic 2.1 The English language in use

Topic vocabulary

Getting started		
periodical [ˌpɪəriˈɒdɪkəl]	Zeitschrift	= publication that comes out e.g. monthly or quarterly
native	Einheimische(r)	e.g. native speaker (= Muttersprachler)
A English as lingua franca		
lingua franca [ˌlɪŋgwɑˈfræŋkə]	internationale Verkehrssprache	= vehicular language
unparalleled [ʌnˈpærəleld]	beispiellos	= unprecedented
scarcely [ˈskeəsli]	kaum	= hardly
to promote	fördern, unterstützen	→ promotion
appeal	Anziehungskraft	= attraction
censorship	Zensur	→ to censor
blog	Internet-Tagebuch	= a diary on the internet
riot	Aufruhr	= uproar
casualty [ˈkæʒjuəlti]	Opfer	= dead person
to perceive [pəˈsiːv]	wahrnehmen	= to see
predominance [prɪˈdɒmɪnəns]	Vorherrschaft	= having power and influence over other groups
unanimous [juːˈnænɪməs]	einhellig, einstimmig	→ unanimity [ˌjuːnəˈnɪməti] (= Einstimmigkeit)
to impose sth.	etw. auferlegen	→ imposition (= Auferlegung, Aufzwingen)
to counter	erwidern, dagegen sprechen	= to argue
advance	Fortschritt	= progress

B The language of tomorrow?		
adviser	Ratgeber(in)	= sb. who gives advice
curriculum [kə'rɪkjələm]	Lehrplan	= subjects one studies at college
compulsory [kəm'pʌlsəri]	vorgeschrieben	= obligatory [ə'blɪgətəri]
requirement	Anforderung	→ to require
random ['rændəm]	per Zufall	= accidental
to succeed	erfolgreich sein	↔ to fail
C Language and immigration		
prospect	Aussicht	→ prospective (= zukünftig)
fluency	Flüssigkeit	→ fluent
pattern	Muster	= trend
roughly	ungefähr	= about
outcome	Ergebnis	= result
decade ['dekeɪd]	Jahrzehnt	→ century (= Jahrhundert)
to anticipate [æn'tɪsɪpeɪt]	erwarten	= to expect
entire	ganz	= whole
emphasis ['emfəsɪs]	Betonung	→ to emphasise
to struggle	sich schwer tun	= to have difficulty with
sufficient [sə'fɪʃənt]	ausreichend	= enough
tie	Bindung	= bond
D Whose English is it anyway?		
manipulation [məˌnɪpjə'leɪʃən]	Beeinflussung	→ to manipulate [mə'nɪpjəleɪt]
E Shakespearian English		
accessible	zugänglich	e.g. wheelchair accessible
bold	mutig, entschlossen	= determined
to secure	absichern	→ security
compelling [kəm'pelɪŋ]	faszinierend	= fascinating

to leap [liːp]	springen	= to jump
venture	Unternehmen, Projekt	e.g. joint venture (= Gemeinschaftsunternehmen)
Spot on language		
negotiation [nɪˌɡəʊʃi'eɪʃən]	Verhandlung	= a formal discussion to reach agreement
Hotspot		
to blend	mischen	= to mix
Exam practice		
to hesitate ['hezɪteɪt]	zögern	= to pause
drill	Übung	= exercise, training
fraction	Bruchteil	= very small part
clumsy ['klʌmzi]	unbeholfen	= not elegant

Additional vocabulary

(sich) anpassen	to adapt	↔ to adopt (etw. annehmen)
hier: etw. anwenden	to employ	e.g. to employ satire
aufgeschlossen	open-minded	= to be open about sth.
Aufmerksamkeit	attention	e.g. to hold sb. attention (= jmdn fesseln)
aussetzen (einer Gefahr, einem Risiko)	to expose	→ exposure [ɪk'spəʊʒə]
behindern	to hinder	= to limit
etw. als Besonderheit ausweisen	to feature ['fiːtʃə] sth.	→ feature (= besonderes Kennzeichen)
Betrug	deceit [dɪ'siːt]	= fraud
Ehrgeiz	ambition	→ ambitious
Ereignis	event	= sth. that happens
erwerben, sich aneignen	to acquire	e.g. to acquire a language
Figur, Gestalt	character	e.g. a character in a film
Gattung	genre ['ʒɑ̃ːrə]	e.g. This book is a classic of the mystery genre.

Gebrauch, Sprachgebrauch	usage	→ to use
glaubwürdig	believable	↔ unbelievable
Handlung	plot	= a series of events that make up a story
Ironie	irony	→ ironic
Lyrik, Poesie	poetry	→ poetic
passend	appropriate [ə'prəʊpriət]	= suitable, fitting
prägen (einen Begriff, eine Münze)	to coin	= to create
Prosa	prose [prəʊz]	e.g. narrative prose (= Erzählprosa)
Redewendung	idiom	= a particular combination of words that does not have the same meaning as the meanings of the individual words
Roman	novel	↔ biography
Romanschriftsteller(in)	novelist	= sb. who writes a novel
Rückblende	flashback	↔ anticipation (= Vorgriff)
Satire	satire ['sætaɪə]	→ satirical
Schauplatz	setting	= scenery
Spannung	suspense	= tension
Sprachgewandtheit	fluency	→ fluent
Stilmittel	device	e.g. stylistic device
Tragödie	tragedy	↔ comedy
Untertreibung	understatement	↔ exaggeration [ɪgˌzædʒər'eɪʃən] (= Übertreibung)
verständlich	comprehensible	= understandable
Zutat, Merkmal	ingredient [ɪn'gri:diənt]	= component
zweisprachig	bilingual	= able to speak two languages fluently

Exercises

a) Word family: Fill in the missing words in the table (no -ing or -ed forms). Use a dictionary and translate them into German.

Noun	Verb	Adjective
– adviser – Ratgeber(in)		
	– to perceive –	
– predominance –		
– deceit –		
		– accessible –
	– to hesitate –	
– negotiation –		
		– comprehensible –

b) Complete the text with the words from below. Two words don't fit!

well-chosen | although | immediately | believable | action | employ
identify | fitting atmosphere | manipulation | ingredients | plot | round
reasons | tension | anticipation | strong opening | tragedy | devices

What are the __________________ (1) of a good novel?

1. An imaginative __________________ (2): the sequence of events must be interesting __________________ (3) it does not have to be chronological (the novelist might decide to include flashbacks or __________________ (4)). Suspense or a twist can create __________________ (5).
2. A __________________ (6) setting: the __________________ (7) must be set in a time and place of interest to the reader. This will in turn help to create a __________________ (8).
3. __________________ (9) characters: the characters should be __________________ (10) and have clear defined personalities and __________________ (11) for what they say and do. The reader should be able to __________________ (12) with some of the characters.
4. A __________________ (13): the first sentence should __________________ (14) hold the reader's attention.
5. Appropriate stylistic __________________ (15): these will make the novel more enjoyable. The novelist can __________________ (16) satire, irony, understatement, etc. to make the novel more interesting.

c) Find the word or expression in each row which does not go with the others and cross it out. Explain your choice.

1.	☐ scarcely	☐ hardly	☐ clumsy
2.	☐ to expose	☐ to argue	☐ to counter
3.	☐ to leap	☐ to impose	☐ to jump
4.	☐ to hinder	☐ to censor	☐ to limit

5.	☐ drill	☐ venture	☐ training
6.	☐ appropriate	☐ suitable	☐ unanimous
7.	☐ suspense	☐ ambition	☐ tension
8.	☐ casualty	☐ accidental	☐ random
9.	☐ scale	☐ extent	☐ requirement
10.	☐ application	☐ attraction	☐ appeal
11.	☐ compulsory	☐ obligatory	☐ unprecedented

d) What's the word in English?

1. mutig: ________________
2. Bindung: ________________
3. Betonung: ________________
4. sich schwer tun: ________________
5. vorgeschrieben: ________________
6. Einheimische(r): ________________
7. Zeitschrift: ________________
8. Anziehungskraft: ________________
9. Fortschritt: ________________
10. erwidern, dagegen sprechen: ________________
11. Opfer: ________________
12. Aufruhr: ________________

e) Translate the clues below and then write the answers in the grid.

1. Lehrplan
2. internationale Verkehrssprache
3. zensieren
4. Internettagebuch
5. sichern
6. etw. als Besonderheit ausweisen
7. Zutat
8. Schauplatz
9. Sprache

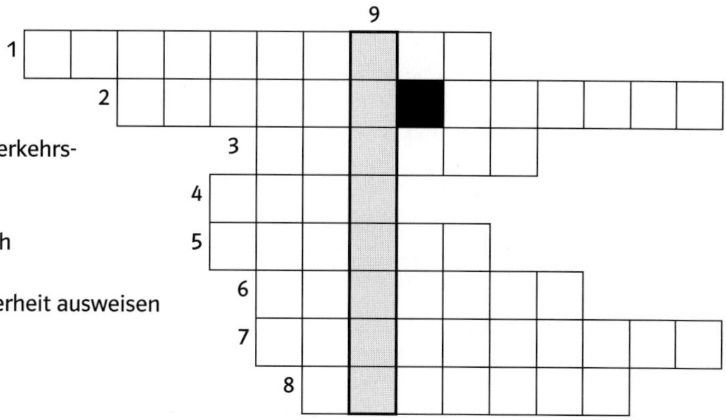

Topic 2.2 The United States – then and now

Topic vocabulary

Getting started		
attainable	erreichbar	= achievable
A The history of the United States		
settler	Siedler(in)	→ settlement
slave	Sklave, Sklavin	e.g. slave labour
segregation	Rassentrennung	= separation of races
to withdraw [wɪð'drɔ:]	sich zurückziehen	→ withdrawal (= Rückzug)
B The American Dream		
reliable	zuverlässig	= dependable
to dishonor [dɪ'sɒnə]	entehren	= to bring shame or disgrace on
self-evident	selbstverständlich	= obvious
betrayal [bɪ'treɪəl]	Verrat, Treuebruch	→ to betray
to marginalize ['mɑ:dʒɪnəlaɪz]	an den Rand drängen	= to treat sb. as a less important social group
C The American political system		
to reject	zurückweisen	→ rejection
to ratify	ratifizieren	e.g. to ratify a treaty
inauguration [ɪˌnɔ:gjə'reɪʃn]	Amtseinführung	= the action of putting sb. in office
applicant	Bewerber(in)	= sb. who formally requests a job
presidency ['prezɪdənsɪ]	Präsidentschaft	= being president of sth.
primary	Vorwahl	= here: an election in the US to find the best candidate

majority [mə'dʒɒrətɪ]	Mehrheit	↔ minority
to veto ['vi:təʊ]	Veto einlegen	e.g to veto a law
D Racial (in)equality		
irreversible [ˌɪrɪ'vɜ:səbl]	unumkehrbar	= impossible to undo
burden	Last	e.g. burden of debts (= Schuldenlast)
substantial	beträchtlich	= considerable
to expel	ausschließen	→ expulsion (= Ausschluss)
infant mortality [ˌɪnfənt mɔ:'tælətɪ]	Kindersterblichkeit	= the death of children under the age of one year
disparity	Ungleichheit	= great difference
deterioration [dɪˌtɪərɪə'reɪʃn]	Verschlechterung	→ to deteriorate
sore	Wunde	e.g. sore throat (= Halsentzündung)
to segregate	trennen	→ segregation
E America's responsibility		
authoritarian [ˌɔ:θɒrɪ'teəriən]	autoritär	e.g. an authoritarian regime
to intervene	einschreiten	→ intervention
oppressive	unterdrückend	= tyrannical
criticism ['krɪtɪsɪzəm]	Kritik	→ critic (= Kritiker/in)
allusion [ə'lu:ʒən]	Anspielung	= hint
Exam practice		
to propose to sb.	jmdm einen Heiratsantrag machen	→ proposition, proposal (= Antrag)
subprime mortgage crisis [ˌsʌbpraɪm‿'mɔ:gɪdʒ ˌkraɪsɪs]	US-Immobilienkrise	= real estate crisis
to foreclose	zwangsvollstrecken	→ foreclosure (= Zwangsvollstreckung)
vacant	frei	→ vacancy (= Leerstelle, freies Zimmer, freie Stelle)
gloomy	düster	= grim

rundown	heruntergekommen	↔ well-kept (= gepflegt)
to revitalize [ˌriːˈvaɪtəlaɪz]	wiederbeleben	= to bring back to life
to commute	pendeln	→ commuter (= Pendler/in)
momentum	Schwung, Dynamik	e.g. to gain momentum
to depreciate [dɪˈpriːʃɪeɪt]	abschreiben	→ depreciation (= Abschreibung)

Additional vocabulary

Abhängigkeit	dependence	= reliance
Abrüstung	disarmament [dɪˈsɑːməmənt]	→ to disarm
befreien	to liberate	→ liberation
befürworten	to advocate	= to support
begreifen	to conceive [kənˈsiːv]	= to understand
bestehen	to persist	e.g. to persist in one's viewpoint (= auf seinem Standpunkt verharren)
bürgerlich	civic	e.g. civic centre (= Regierungszentrum)
Demütigung	humiliation [hjuːˌmɪlɪˈeɪʃn]	→ to humiliate
Einfluss	influence	= impact, effect
Einmarsch	invasion	→ to invade
Einmischung	interference	→ to interfere
entschärfen	to de-escalate [ˌdiːˈeskəleɪt]	e.g. to de-escalate tensions
Epoche, Ära	era [ˈɪərə]	= age
etw. finanzieren	to fund sth.	= to finance sth.
Gefangene(r)	captive [ˈkæptɪv]	= prisoner
intervenieren	to intervene	→ interventionism [ˌɪntəˈvenʃənɪzəm]
isolieren	to isolate	→ isolationism [ˌaɪsəˈleɪʃənɪzəm]
kurz und bündig	concise [kənˈsaɪs]	e.g. a concise explanation
raten	to advise	→ advice (= Ratschlag)

Schmelztiegel	melting pot	→ to melt (= schmelzen)
Staatsvertrag	treaty	= an official written agreement between states
gegen etw. stimmen	to vote against sth.	e.g. Congress voted against signing the Treaty of Versailles.
tragen	to bear [beə]	→ bearable (= erträglich)
verhandeln	to negotiate [nɪˈgəʊʃieɪt]	= to bargain
verwurzelt	ingrained [ɪnˈgreɪnd]	= deep-rooted
weltlich	secular	↔ religious

Exercises

a) Which of the following verbs and nouns can be combined? Sometimes you might have to add an article or preposition. Then translate the expressions into German.

friend captive minorities contract student
neighbourhood troops ✓ machine arms work

to withdraw *troops*	Truppen zurückziehen
to depreciate	
to revitalize	
to negotiate	
to expel	
to liberate	
to commute	
to betray	
to marginalize	
to bear	

b) **Word family: Fill in the missing words in the table (no -ing or -ed forms). Use a dictionary and translate them into German.**

Noun	Verb	Adjective
		– attainable – erreichbar
		– reliable –
	– to persist –	
– dependence –		
– influence –		

c) **What's the word in English?**

1. Vorwahl: ____________________
2. Bewerber(in): ____________________
3. Amtseinführung: ____________________
4. entehren: ____________________
5. Siedler(in): ____________________
6. frei: ____________________
7. zwangsvollstrecken: ____________________
8. jmdm einen Heiratsantrag machen: ____________________
9. Anspielung: ____________________
10. selbstverständlich: ____________________
11. Rassentrennung: ____________________
12. ratifizieren: ____________________
13. US-Immobilienkrise: ____________________
14. einschreiten: ____________________
15. Last: ____________________
16. Ungleichheit: ____________________

d) Translate the clues below and then write the answers in the grid.

Across
3. kurz und bündig
4. Sklave
6. entehren
8. Wunde
9. frei
10. begreifen
14. verwurzelt
15. Abrüstung
16. Staatsvertrag

Down
1. weltlich
2. Einmarsch
5. zwangsvollstrecken
7. Demütigung
11. bestehen
12. raten
13. düster

Topic 2.3 The United Kingdom – then and now

Topic vocabulary

Getting started		
to apologise [ə'pɒlədʒaɪz]	sich entschuldigen	→ apology (= Entschuldigung)
inconvenience [ˌɪnkən'viːniəns]	Unannehmlichkeit	→ inconvenient
freedom	Freiheit	e.g. freedom of speech (= Redefreiheit)
CCTV [ˌsisiti'vi]	Videoüberwachung	= closed circuit televison
A The British Empire and the Commonwealth		
hence	daher, deshalb	= therefore
foremost	führend	= leading
to gain	erhalten, bekommen	= to get
to conquer	besiegen	→ conquest
to aid	helfen	= to help, to support
indigenous [ɪn'dɪdʒɪnəs] people	Einheimische	= natives
urge [ɜːdʒ]	Drang, Trieb	= a strong desire
civil service	Beamtentum, öffentlicher Dienst	e.g. a civil service career
prejudice ['predʒədɪs]	Vorurteil	e.g. racial prejudice
to lessen sth.	etw. verringern	= to reduce
feasible ['fiːzəbl]	machbar	→ feasibility (= Machbarkeit)
B Britishness		
issue ['ɪʃuː]	Thema	= topic
mosque [mɒsk]	Moschee	= Islamic place of worship
despite	trotz	= in spite of

fragile ['frædʒaɪl]	zerbrechlich, schwach	→ fragility
appeal	Anreiz	= attraction
C The British political system		
constitution	Verfassung	→ constitutional
judiciary [dʒuː'dɪʃərɪ]	Gerichtsbarkeit	→ legislative ['ledʒɪslətɪv], executive [ɪg'zekjətɪv]
commander-in-chief	Oberbefehlshaber	= sb. who commands all forces in a country
constituency [kən'stɪtjʊənsɪ]	Wahlbezirk	→ constituent (= Wähler/in)
to appoint	ernennen, verpflichten	= to make sb. responsible for sth.
to be in charge of sth.	zuständig sein für etw.	= to be responsible for sth.
Secretary of State (AE)	Außenminister(in)	= Foreign Secretary (BE)
Secretary of the Interior [ɪn'tɪəriə] (AE)	Innenminister(in)	= Home Secretary (BE)
Secretary of Treasury	Finanzminister(in)	= Chancellor of the Exchequer [ɪks'tʃekə]
assembly	Versammlung	→ to assemble
to favour sth.	etw. bevorzugen	↔ to disadvantage sth.
D The Royal Family		
affection	Zuneigung	→ to be affected to
capable ['keɪpəbl]	fähig	→ capability
to reinforce	verstärken	→ reinforcement (= Verstärkung)
tension ['tenʃn]	Spannung	→ tense (= angespannt)
to distinguish [dɪ'stɪŋgwɪʃ]	unterscheiden	= to differentiate
doomed	verdammt	= cursed
evident	offensichtlich	→ evidence (= Beweis)
E Britain and Europe		
entirely	vollständig	= completely
to purchase ['pɜːtʃəs]	erwerben	→ the purchase

to govern	leiten, lenken, regieren	e.g. to govern a country
to implement	einführen, umsetzen	→ implementation
to deploy	einsetzen	→ deployment (= Einsatz)
to impose	auferlegen	→ imposition (= Auferlegung)
likelihood	Wahrscheinlichkeit	→ likely
overseas	ausländisch	= foreign
GDP	Bruttoinlandsprodukt	= gross domestic product
proponent [prəˈpəʊnənt]	Befürworter(in)	↔ opponent
to boost [buːst]	in die Höhe treiben	= to increase
to rely on	sich verlassen auf	→ reliance (= Verlass)
to regard	betrachten	= to consider
Exam practice		
row	Auseinandersetzung	= fight
to remain	bleiben	e.g. Please remain seated.
malnourished [ˌmælˈnʌrɪʃt]	unterernährt	→ malnutrition (= Unterernährung)
disparity [dɪˈspærəti]	Ungleichheit	= inequality
accusation	Anschuldigung	→ to accuse
violation	Verletzung, Nichteinhaltung	→ to violate
to promote	fördern	→ promotion
expenditure [ɪkˈspendɪtʃə]	Ausgaben, Auslagen	= money spent
benefit	Nutzen, Vorteil	= advantage
to terminate	beenden	→ termination
to acknowledge	anerkennen	→ acknowledgement (= Anerkennung)
exploitation [ˌeksplɔɪˈteɪʃn]	Ausbeutung	→ to exploit
beneficial [ˌbenɪˈfɪʃl]	nützlich, förderlich	= useful

Additional vocabulary

Abschaffung des Kolonialismus	decolonization [ˌdi:kɒlɪnaɪ'zeɪʃn]	↔ colonization
Angelegenheiten	affairs	e.g. foreign affairs
Anpassung	adjustment [ə'dʒʌstmənt]	= a change made
Anwendung, Bewerbung	application	→ to apply
Bemühungen, Anstrengungen	endeavour [ɪn'devə]	e.g. imperial endeavour
Förderung, Ermunterung	encouragement	↔ discouragement
gegen etw. sein	to oppose sth.	→ opposition
Herrschaft	reign [reɪn]	→ to reign
Kolonie	colony	e.g. Crown Colony
Konservative Partei	Conservative Party (Tories)	↔ Labour Party, Liberal Democrats
konstitutionelle Monarchie	constitutional monarchy [ˌkɒnstɪ'tju:ʃənəl 'mɒnəkɪ]	e.g. Great Britain
Legislaturperiode	legislative ['ledʒɪslətɪv] period	→ legislation (= Gesetzgebung)
Mehrheitswahlrecht	first-past-the-post system	= majority voting system
englisches Oberhaus	House of Lords	↔ House of Commons
parlamentarische Demokratie	parliamentary democracy [ˌpɑ:lə'mentərɪ dɪ'mɒkrəsɪ]	= democracy where all power is held by the parliament
Parlamentsabgeordnete(r)	Member of Parliament	= MP
Premierminister(in)	Prime Minister	= PM
eine Regierung bilden	to form a government	↔ to dismiss a government
Schutzgebiet, Protektorat	protectorate [prə'tektərət]	→ to protect
Siedlung in Übersee	overseas settlement ['setlmənt]	→ to settle
Staatsoberhaupt	head of state	e.g. King/Queen or President
unabhängiger Staat	sovereign ['sɒvərɪn] state	→ sovereignty ['sɒvrəntɪ]
die Unabhängigkeit erlangen	to gain independence	= to become independent
hier: Untertan	subject	compare: citizen (= Staatsbürger)

Verwaltung	administration	→ to administrate, administrative
die Wähler, Wählerschaft	electorate [ɪ'lektərət]	→ to elect, election
wahlberechtigt sein	to be eligible to vote ['elɪdʒəbl]	→ eligibility [ˌelɪdʒə'bɪlətɪ]

Exercises

a) Word family: Fill in the missing words in the table (no -ing or -ed forms). Use a dictionary and translate them into German.

Noun	Verb	Adjective
– adjustment – Anpassung		
	– to govern –	
– urge –		
		– oppressive –
– colony –		

b) What's the word in English?

1. Videoüberwachung: ____________
2. führend: ____________
3. Vorurteil: ____________
4. Gerichtsbarkeit: ____________
5. englisches Oberhaus: ____________
6. Staatsoberhaupt: ____________
7. Legislaturperiode: ____________
8. Ermunterung, Förderung: ____________
9. Mehrheitswahlrecht: ____________
10. eingefleischt, verwurzelt: ____________
11. Herrschaft: ____________
12. Befürworter(in): ____________

c) Find the words in this topic that match these definitions.

1. sb. who was born in monarchy: ____________________
2. sb. who works for the government: ____________________
3. possible to do: ____________________
4. clear to see: ____________________
5. to make stronger: ____________________
6. to beat in battle: ____________________
7. the total value of goods and services that is produced by a nation: ____________________
8. having the qualities to do sth.: ____________________
9. to be against sth.: ____________________
10. gentle feeling of fondness or liking: ____________________
11. to depend on: ____________________
12. to recognise: ____________________

d) Find the word or expression in each row which does not go with the others and cross it out. Explain your choice.

1.	☐ constitutional monarchy	☐ Prime Minister	☐ parliamentary democracy
2.	☐ to become	☐ to get	☐ to gain
3.	☐ to lessen	☐ to reduce	☐ to conquer
4.	☐ to reinforce	☐ to aid	☐ to help
5.	☐ entirely	☐ completely	☐ evident
6.	☐ doomed	☐ ethnic	☐ cursed
7.	☐ affairs	☐ notion	☐ idea
8.	☐ since	☐ as	☐ subject
9.	☐ advantage	☐ benefit	☐ application
10.	☐ disparity	☐ strain	☐ inequality

e) Complete the text with the words from below.

symbolic | links | equal | exclusive | to join | application

encouragement | to oppose | cultural activities | particularly

role | formerly | independent | to be part of | human rights

The Commonwealth of Nations

The Commonwealth of Nations, ________________ (1) the British Commonwealth of Nations, is an association of 53 ________________ (2) nations, plus several British dependencies such as Bermuda, the Falkland Islands and Gibraltar. Most members used ________________ (3) the British Empire. Any nation wishing ________________ (4) the Commonwealth must be independent, and its ________________ (5) must be acceptable to existing members. The ________________ (6) head of the Commonwealth is the British monarch. Members of the Commonwealth have special ________________ (7) with the United Kingdom and with each other. All members are ________________ (8) and agree to work together towards world peace, the ____________________________ (9) of trade, the defence of democracy and improvements in ____________________________ (10), health and education. During World War II, Commonwealth forces played an important ________________ (11) in the war effort. Critics say that the Commonwealth is pointless or little more than an ________________ (12) club. However, Commonwealth nations united ________________ (13) apartheid in South Africa, and they also encourage joint ____________________________ (14) and sports events, ________________ (15) the Commonwealth Games, which are held every four years.

Topic 2.4 World of work

Topic vocabulary

Getting started		
confident	sicher, selbstbewusst	→ confidence
A Applying for a job		
résumé ['rezju:meɪ]	Lebenslauf	= American English for CV
application	Bewerbung	e.g. letter of application (= Bewerbungsschreiben)
recommendation	Empfehlung	e.g. a letter of recommendation
sample	Beispiel	= an example
to gather	sammeln	= to collect
objective	Absicht	= intention
trait [treɪ]	Charakterzug	= characteristic
to verify	belegen	→ verification
to reject	ablehnen	= to turn down
to comply with	übereinstimmen mit	= to agree with
survey ['sɜ:veɪ]	Umfrage	→ to survey
confidential	vertraulich	= private, secret
appreciation [əˌpri:ʃi'eɪʃən]	Wertschätzung	→ to appreciate
B Work placements		
to denounce	verurteilen	= publicly declare to be wrong and evil
debt [det]	Schuld, Schulden	= the money you owe
well-to-do	wohlhabend	= wealthy
to exploit	ausbeuten	→ exploitation
to donate	spenden	→ donation
to assess	beurteilen	→ assessment

accommodation [əˌkɒmə'deɪʃən]	Unterbringung	→ to accommodate
to pursue [pə'sjuː]	verfolgen	→ pursuit (= Streben)
loan	Darlehen, Kredit	= the money you borrow
to accelerate	beschleunigen	= to go faster
C Teenage unemployment		
peak	Höchststand	e.g. to hit a peak
vacancy ['veɪkənsi]	freie Stelle	→ vacant
to encourage	ermutigen	↔ discourage
to tackle sth.	etw. angehen	e.g. to tackle a problem
youth charity	Jugendhilfsorganisation	→ charitable
vulnerable ['vʌlnərəbl]	verletzlich	= can be hurt easily
tuition [tju'ɪʃən]	Unterricht, Unterweisung	e.g. tuition fees (= Studiengebühren)
D Corporate culture		
to lack sth.	etw. vermissen lassen	→ lack (= der Mangel)
unanimously [juː'nænɪməsli]	einstimmig	→ unanimity
handicapped	Behinderte(r)	= disabled
to act on sth.	auf etw. reagieren	= to react on sth.
despite	trotz	= in spite of
hyphen	Bindestrich	= dash
suspicion [sə'spɪʃən]	Verdacht	→ suspicious (= verdächtig)
doubt [daʊt]	Zweifel	= uncertainty
dull	langweilig	= boring
E Job satisfaction		
generous ['dʒenərəs]	großzügig	→ generosity
gorgeous ['gɔːdʒəs]	sehr schön	= beautiful
praise [preɪz]	Lob	→ to praise

to bother	sich die Mühe machen	= to make an effort
sincere [sɪn'sɪə]	aufrichtig	↔ insincere
accomplishment [ə'kʌmplɪʃmənt]	Leistung	= achievement
honesty ['ɒnɪsti]	Aufrichtigkeit	↔ dishonesty
crucial ['kru:ʃəl]	entscheidend	= decisive
core	Kern	e.g. core business (= Kerngeschäft)
capability	Fähigkeit	= ability
recipe ['resɪpi]	Rezept	↔ prescription (= Verordnung eines Arztes)
to urge [ɜ:dʒ]	drängen	= to strongly recommend
inconvenience [ˌɪnkən'vi:niəns]	Unannehmlichkeit	→ inconvenient
Spot on language		
pattern	Muster	= a particular way in which sth. is done
guardian	Erziehungsberechtigte(r)	= formal for parents
Exam practice		
to reckon	vermuten	= to suppose
high-flying	erfolgreich	= very successful
to commission sth.	etw. in Auftrag geben	= to officially ask sb. to do sth.
in demand	gesucht	→ demand
remote working	Telearbeit	= telework
gain	Gewinn	→ to gain
disability	Behinderung	→ disabled
solicitor [sə'lɪsɪtə]	Anwalt, Anwältin	= a type of lawyer in Britain
supervision	Aufsicht	→ to supervise

Additional vocabulary

Angestellte(r)	white-collar worker	↔ blue-collar worker
Arbeitnehmer(in)	employee	↔ employer
Arbeitslosigkeit	unemployment	→ unemployed, out-of-work
attraktiv	appealing	= attractive
beilegen	to enclose	→ enclosure
bezahlte Krankheitstage	paid sick leave	→ to be off sick (= wegen Krankheit fehlen)
echt	genuine ['dʒenjuɪn]	↔ fake
eifrig	eager ['i:gə]	= willing
jmdn entlassen	to lay sb. off	= to fire, to sack, to make redundant
Errungenschaft	achievement	→ to achieve
Erwerb	acquisition	→ to acquire
Fähigkeit	aptitude ['æptɪtju:d]	= ability
Festanstellung	permanent position	↔ temporary position
freiberuflich tätig werden	to go freelance ['fri:lɑ:ns]	→ freelancer
gedeihen, florieren	to prosper	= to thrive, to flourish
Gehalt	salary	e.g. to pay a salary
genug, genügend, ausreichend	sufficient	= enough
Gewerkschaft	trade union (BE)	= labor union (AE)
Gleichberechtigung	equality	= the state of being equal
Karriere	career	e.g. good career prospects
Kollege, Kollegin	colleague ['kɒli:g]	= co-worker
näher ausführen	to elaborate	= to explain
obligatorisch	compulsory [kəm'pʌlsərɪ]	↔ optional
Rentenalter	retirement age	→ to retire
Selbstvertrauen	self-confidence	→ self-confident
Stärke	strength [streŋθ]	↔ weakness
sich auf eine Stelle bewerben	to apply for a job	→ application, applicant
Überstunden	overtime	e.g. overtime rates

umfassend	comprehensive [ˌkɒmprɪˈhensɪv]	= extensive
ungelernt	unskilled	↔ skilled
Vorstellungsgespräch	job interview	→ to interview

Exercises

a) Word family: Fill in the missing words in the table (no -ing or -ed forms). Use a dictionary and translate them into German.

Noun	Verb	Adjective
– application – Bewerbung, Anwendung		
– recommendation –		
– strength –		
	– to accelerate –	– – –
– equality –		
		– sufficient –
– doubt –		

b) Find the word or expression in each row which does not go with the others. Explain your choice.

1.	☐ appealing	☐ dull	☐ attractive
2.	☐ to explain	☐ to elaborate	☐ to exploit
3.	☐ to pursue	☐ to thrive	☐ to prosper
4.	☐ to sack	☐ to lay off	☐ to retire
5.	☐ to urge	☐ to reject	☐ to turn down
6.	☐ to verify	☐ to suppose	☐ to reckon

7.	☐ crucial	☐ eager	☐ decisive
8.	☐ dull	☐ despite	☐ boring
9.	☐ gorgeous	☐ generous	☐ beautiful

c) **Complete the text with the words from below. Two words don't fit!**

appearance achievements employer potential knowledge
self-confidence key part, preparation interview impression
commit proper strengths state beforehand

Competitive interview ______________ (1)

Preparation is a ______________ (2) of any interview process. However, many do not ______________ (3) enough time. Remember, you only have one chance to make a good ______________ (4)! Follow these steps in order to be ______________ (5) prepared:

1. Know your ______________ (6) – Find out as much as possible about the company: its products, its structure and if possible recent ______________ (7).
2. Know yourself – Evaluate yourself in terms of ______________ (8), and how your future employer could use them. If you need to ______________ (9) a weakness, do not elaborate on it and try to turn it into a ______________ (10) strength.
3. Communicate effectively – If you can't communicate your ______________ (11) clearly, your interview will not be impressive. The best way to improve your communication skills and ______________ (12) is to practice role-playing ______________ (13).
4. Be careful about the so-called "soft skills" – If you are looking for a professional ______________ (14), you must look like a professional. Therefore, a neat, clean ______________ (15), polished shoes and a neat hairdo are essential.
5. Finally, be on time – It's always better to be a few minutes early than one minute late for your ______________ (16). So ______________ (17) you know how to get to the interview and how long the journey takes.

d) Complete the text with the verbs from below. Two verbs don't fit!

are required | are seeking | to work | must be
have | send | is | is required | seek

MHS PLASTICS
(REF.: ET 102)

We ________________ (1) enthusiastic individuals from the Continent ________________ (2) in our Manchester-based export team.

Applicants ________________ (3) educated to A Level standard or equivalent and ________________ (4) excellent communication skills. Native speaker competence in Italian, French or German and good English language skills ________________ (5).

An initial one year package ________________ (6) on offer including comprehensive training, good rates of pay, challenging and interesting work leading to a permanent position.

________________ (7) application enclosing CV and certificates in English to:

Roberta Burns, Recruitment officer, MHS Plastics Ltd, 67 High Street,
Manchester, M1 2HF

Topic 2.5 Science, technology and society

Topic vocabulary

Getting started		
side effect	Nebenwirkung	e.g. Some people take pills without considering side effects.
hazard ['hæzəd]	Gefahr	→ hazardous (= gefährlich)
surgery ['sɜ:dʒəri]	Operation	e.g. minimally invasive [ɪn'veɪsɪv] surgery (= minimalinvasive Operationstechnik)
power plant [plɑ:nt]	Kraftwerk	e.g. a nuclear power plant
solar panel [ˌsəʊlə 'pænəl]	Sonnenkollektor	→ solar energy
double-edged sword [sɔ:d]	zweischneidiges Schwert	= sth. having both advantages and disadvantages
A Genetics		
genetic engineering [dʒəˌnetɪk endʒɪ'nɪərɪŋ]	Genforschung	→ genetic modification (= Genveränderung)
insurance	Versicherung	e.g. insurance policy (= Versicherungsschein)
to clone	klonen	→ a clone
healthcare	Gesundheitspflege	→ healthcare system (= Gesundheitswesen)
embryonic [ˌembri'ɒnɪk]	Embryo-	→ embryo
approval [ə'pru:vəl]	Zustimmung	↔ disapproval
spinal cord ['spaɪnəl ˌkɔ:d]	Rückenmark	→ spinal disc (= Bandscheibe)
curative ['kjʊərətɪv]	heilend	= able to heal
fertility [fə'tɪləti]	Fruchtbarkeit	e.g. fertility treatment (= Behandlung gegen Unfruchtbarkeit)

to predict	voraussagen	= to say that sth. will happen in the future
tissue ['tɪʃu:]	Gewebe	e.g. nerve tissue
B Human spare parts		
flattering ['flætərɪŋ]	schmeichelhaft	→ to flatter (= schmeicheln)
relapse ['ri:læps]	Rückfall	= return of an illness
D Smart homes		
surface ['sɜ:fɪs]	Oberfläche	= the level top of sth.
sophisticated [sə'fɪstɪkeɪtɪd]	hoch entwickelt	e.g. a sophisticated machine
monitoring	Überwachung	= supervision
bone	Knochen	e.g. bone marrow (= Knochenmark)
E The next fifty years		
prediction [prɪ'dɪkʃən]	Vorhersage	= forecast for the future
laboratory [lə'bɒrətəri]	Labor	= a room with scientific equipment
to enhance	verbessern	= to improve
to strengthen	stärken	= to make stronger
agenda [ə'dʒendə]	Tagesordnung	e.g. agenda item (= Tagesordnungspunkt)
surveillance [sɜ:'veɪləns]	Überwachung	e.g. surveillance camera
to compute [kəm'pju:t]	rechnen	= to calculate
recognition [ˌrekəg'nɪʃən]	Erkennung	e.g. voice recognition (= Spracherkennung)
intruder [ɪn'tru:də]	Eindringling	→ intrusion (= das Eindringen)
scale ['skeɪl]	Maß, Maßstab	= extent
to impair	beeinträchtigen	e.g. hearing impaired (= hörgeschädigt)

Exam practice (Bundesausgabe)		
to monitor ['mɒnɪtə]	beobachten, überwachen	→ monitor
devastating	verheerend	→ devastation (= Verwüstung, Verheerung)
susceptible to	anfällig für	= prone to

Additional vocabulary

abtreiben	to abort	→ abortion
gegen etw. allergisch sein	to be allergic to sth.	→ allergy
anfällig für etw. sein	to be vulnerable ['vʌlnərəbl] to sth.	→ vulnerability
degenerative Krankheit	degenerative [dɪ'dʒenərətɪv] illness	e.g. Parkinson disease
DNA (früher: DNS)	DNA	= deoxyribonucleic acid
drahtlose Kommunikation	wireless communication	e.g. a cell(ular) phone (AE) or mobile phone (BE)
etw. in etw. einpflanzen	to implant sth. into sth.	→ an implant, implantation
etw. entziffern	to decode sth.	↔ to encode
etw. (von jmdm) erben	to inherit sth. (from sb.)	→ inheritance (= das Erbe)
erblich	hereditary [hɪ'redɪtərɪ]	e.g. hereditary disease
Ethik	ethics ['eθɪks]	→ ethical
Feldfrucht, Nutzpflanze	crop	e.g. corn, wheat
fötal	foetal ['fi:təl]	→ foetus
Forscher(in)	researcher	→ to do research
sich fortpflanzen, züchten	to breed	→ a breeder (= Züchter/in)
Genetik	genetics [dʒə'netɪks]	→ genetic engineering
etw. gentechnisch verändern	to modify sth. genetically	→ genetically modified
gentechnisch verändert	GM	= genetically modified
Impfstoff	vaccine ['væksi:n]	→ to vaccinate
kreuzen	to cross	e.g. to cross species

künstliche Befruchtung	in vitro fertilization [ɪnˈviːtrəʊ ˌfɜːtɪlaɪˈzeɪʃən]	= a technique in which egg cells are fertilised by sperm outside the woman's womb
langfristige Auswirkung	long-term effect	↔ short-term effect
Missbildung	malformation [ˌmælfɔːˈmeɪʃən]	e.g. bone malformation
mutierend, Mutant	mutant (adj/noun) [ˈmjuːtənt]	e.g. a mutant gene
Nährstoffe	nutrients [ˈnjuːtrɪənts]	→ nutrition (= Ernährung)
Nahrungskette	food chain	= describes the feeding relationships between species in an ecological community
obligatorisch	mandatory	= compulsory
Protein	protein [ˈprəʊtiːn]	= a substance that exists in food and helps to keep your body strong
raffiniert, anspruchsvoll	sophisticated [səˈfɪstɪkeɪtɪd]	= refined
etw. regulieren	to regulate sth.	↔ to deregulate
Robotertechnik	robotics	→ robot
Säugetier	mammal [ˈmæməl]	e.g. a sheep
Schädling	pest	→ pesticide (= Schädlings-bekämpfungsmittel)
sexuelle Fortpflanzung	sexual reproduction	→ reproductive technology
Spender(in)	donor	→ to donate, donation
Störung	disorder	e.g. genetic disorder
therapeutisches Klonen	therapeutic [ˌθerəˈpjuːtɪk] cloning	= refers to a procedure which produces cells and organs for medical purposes
Transplantat	transplant	→ to transplant
Unkraut	weed [wiːd]	= a wild plant that grows where it is not wanted
Unkrautvernichtungsmittel	herbicide [ˈhɜːbɪsaɪd]	e.g. herbicide resistant
Unterernährung	malnutrition [ˌmælnjuːˈtrɪʃən]	= illness caused by not having enough food

etw. mit etw. verschmelzen	to fuse sth. with sth.	→ fusion
Widerstandsfähigkeit gegen etw.	resistance to sth.	→ resistant

Exercises

a) Word family: Fill in the missing words in the table (no -ing or -ed forms). Use a dictionary and translate them into German.

Noun	Verb	Adjective
		- mutant - mutierend
	- to donate -	- - -
		- curative -
		- hereditary -
- resistance -		

b) Find words in this topic that match these definitions or synonyms.

1. a medical treatment for couples who have difficulties getting pregnant: ______
2. the amount of profits/crops you get: ______
3. groups of connected cells that humans, animals and plants are made of: ______
4. sb. who enters illegally: ______
5. to observe: ______
6. operation in a hospital: ______
7. to make a copy of a person or animal: ______
8. a building where energy is produced: ______
9. someone who invites people to a meal or party or to stay in their home: ______
10. dangerous: ______

c) Complete the word web with words or phrases from below.

conservation | benefit | malnutrition | unknown effect | pests

safety | enhanced | food allergies | poisonous | mandatory

breed | nutrients | contaminated | benefits | crops

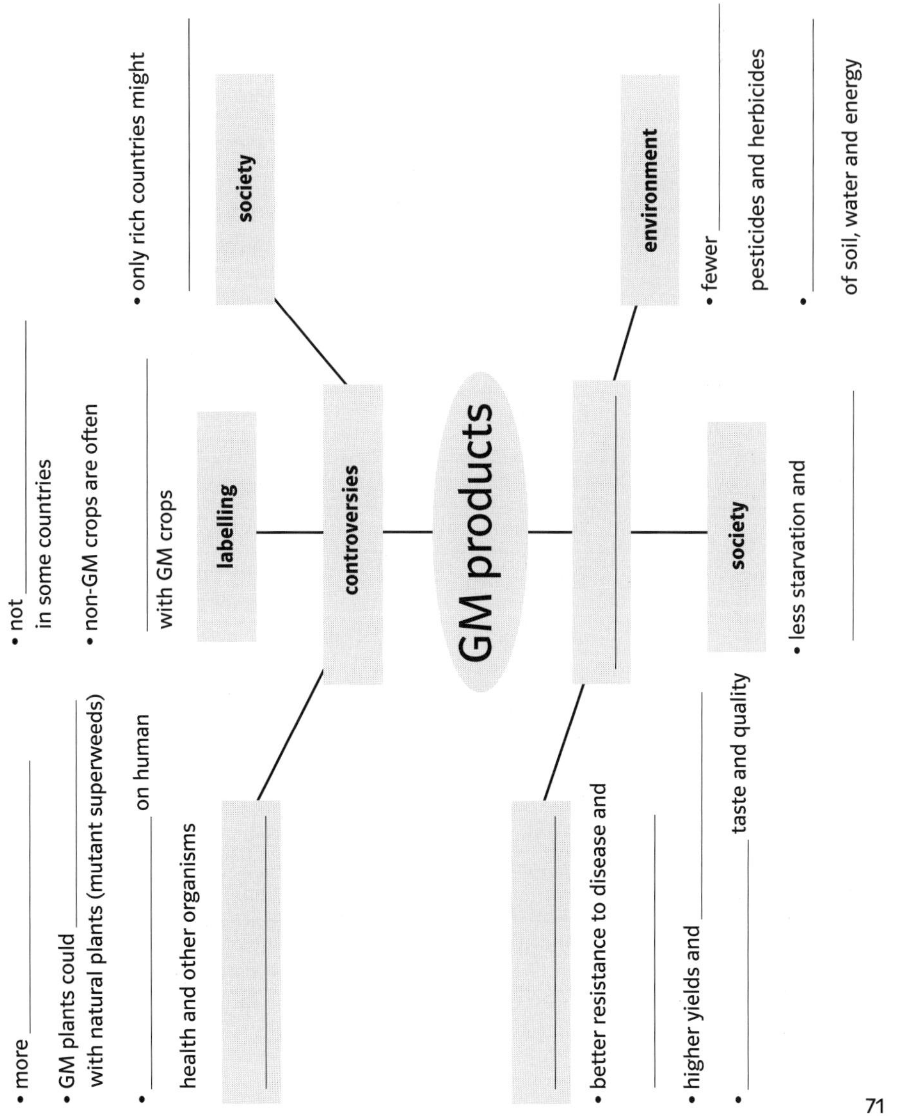

Topic 2.6 The impact of change

Topic vocabulary

Getting started		
impact	Wirkung, Einfluss	→ to impact
storage ['stɔːrɪdʒ]	Speicherung, Lagerung	→ to store
groundbreaking	bahnbrechend	= innovative
innovation	Neuerung	e.g. innovation centre
A Convenience food		
convenience [kən'viːniəns]	Annehmlichkeit, Bequemlichkeit	→ convenient
to consume	verbrauchen	→ consumption
habit	Gewohnheit	→ habitual (= gewöhnlich)
need	Bedürfnis	e.g. Sleeping and eating are basic human needs.
ready-made	Fertig-	= ready to be used
gist [dʒɪst]	Kernaussage	= essence
reputation [ˌrepjə'teɪʃən]	Ruf	e.g. The company has a reputation for quality products.
gravy	(Braten-)Soße	= a kind of sauce
to pave the way	den Weg ebnen	→ to pave (= pflastern, befestigen)
attitude ['ætɪtjuːd]	Haltung	e.g. to adopt an attitude (= eine Haltung einnehmen)
woeful ['wəʊfəl]	traurig	= sad
manufacturer [ˌmænjə'fæktʃərə]	Hersteller(in)	→ to manufacture
merchant	Händler(in)	→ merchandise (= Handelswaren)

to bear [beə] in mind	beachten	= not to forget
to spoil	verderben	= to ruin
value	Wert	e.g. If you add value, sth. becomes more important.
to target	ins Visier nehmen	→ target (= Ziel)
chore [tʃɔ:]	lästige Pflicht	e.g. household chores (= Hausarbeit)
perishable ['perɪʃəbl]	verderblich	e.g. Fruit is perishable.
ingredient [ɪn'gri:diənt]	Zutat	e.g. baking ingredients
to bother ['bɒðə]	sich die Mühe machen	→ to bother sb. (= jmdn belästigen, nerven)
founder	Gründer(in)	→ to found
fish fingers	Fischstäbchen	= frozen fish with bread-crumbs
patriotism ['pætriətɪzm]	Vaterlandsliebe	→ patriotic
to outweigh sth. [ˌaʊt'weɪ]	schwerer wiegen als etw.	e.g. The advantages outweigh the disadvantages.
B Lifelong learning		
dependency [dɪ'pendənsi]	Abhängigkeit	= addiction
guidance ['gaɪdəns]	Ratschläge	→ to guide (= leiten, lenken)
the latter ['lætə]	Letztere(r/s)	= the last in a list
purpose ['pɜ:pəs]	Zweck, Absicht	→ on purpose (= absichtlich)
charity ['tʃærɪti]	Wohltätigkeitsorganisation	→ charitable (= wohltätig)
stroke [strəʊk]	Schlaganfall	e.g. heat stroke (= Hitzschlag)
exaggeration [ɪgˌzædʒər'eɪʃən]	Übertreibung	→ to exaggerate
to deny	verleugnen	→ denial (= Ablehnung)
reliance [rɪ'laɪəns]	Verlass	= depending on sth. for help
C Health education		
scope	Ausmaß, Umfang	= range
conscious ['kɒnʃəs]	bewusst	→ consciousness ['kɒnʃəsnəs]

assortment [ə'sɔːtmənt]	Sortiment, Kollektion	= a range of
thirst [θɜːst]	Durst	→ thirsty
D Digital media		
native	Ureinwohner(in)	e.g. native Americans
to transform	umwandeln	= to change completely
essential	notwendig, wesentlich	= absolutely necessary
instant	sofortig	= immediate
to rule	herrschen	→ ruler (= Herrscher/in)
scary	Angst machend, erschreckend	= frightening
engaging	einnehmend, faszinierend	= fascinating
interface	Schnittstelle	e.g. a virtual interface
pace	Geschwindigkeit	= speed
E New TV culture		
surveillance [sə'veɪləns]	Überwachung	e.g. surveillance camera
poll	Umfrage	e.g. opinion poll
to deny	verweigern	→ denial (= Verweigerung, Bestreiten)
genuine ['dʒenjʊɪn]	echt, aufrichtig	= real, honest
Exam practice		
compulsory [kəm'pʌlsəri]	obligatorisch, vorgeschrieben	= obligatory
retirement	Ruhestand	→ to retire
gentle [dʒentl]	sanft	↔ rough
sensible	vernünftig, sinnvoll	↔ sensitive (= sensibel)

Additional vocabulary

Abonnement	subscription [səb'skrɪpʃn]	e.g. subscription fee
jmdn ansprechen	to appeal to sb.	→ the appeal (= Anreiz)
Ausgabe	edition	→ editor (= Redakteur/in)
beeinflussen	to influence	= to have an impact
Berechnung	calculation	e.g. spreadsheet calculation (= Tabellenkalkulation)
Berichterstattung	coverage	e.g. balanced (= ausgewogene) coverage
Betriebssystem	operating system	e.g. Windows 8
Boulevardpresse	gutter press	→ gutter (= Gosse)
Eigentümer(in)	proprietor [prə'praɪətə]	= owner
Einnahmen	revenue ['revənju:]	e.g. to generate revenue
finanzieren	to fund	= to finance
etw. für Werbezwecke finanzieren	to sponsor sth.	→ the sponsor
Fortschritt	advance	e.g. technological advance
Gebühr	fee	e.g. licence fee
gründlich, in die Tiefe gehend	in-depth [ˌɪn'depθ]	↔ superficial
in jmds Privatsphäre eindringen	to invade sb.'s privacy	→ invasion
Klatsch	gossip ['gɒsɪp]	e.g. gossip column (= Klatschspalte)
Kleinanzeige	classified ad	→ classified section (= Anzeigenteil)
komplex	complex	↔ simple
Masche, Trend, Mode	hype [haɪp]	→ to hype sth. (= etw. aufbauschen)
sachlich	factual	→ fact
Schlagzeile	headline	e.g. attention-grabbing headlines
etw. senden	to broadcast sth.	e.g. broadcasting company (= Rundfunk-/Fernsehanstalt)

seriöse Zeitung	quality newspaper	↔ popular newspaper/ tabloid ['tæblɔɪd]
umfangreich, groß	large-scale	↔ small-scale
veraltet	obsolete ['ɒbsəli:t]	= out-dated
veröffentlichen	to publish	→ publisher
verurteilen	to condemn	→ condemnation
voreingenommen	biased ['baɪəst]	→ to bias sb. (= jmdn beeinflussen)
Werbespot	commercial break	→ commercial (= Werbespot)

Exercises

a) **Word family: Fill in the missing words in the table (no -ing or -ed forms). Use a dictionary and translate them into German.**

Noun	Verb	Adjective
– edition, editor – Ausgabe, Redakteur(in)		
– innovation –		
– regret –		
	– to volunteer –	
– value –		
		– perishable –
– influence –		

b) Complete the text with the words from below.

funded | spends | influential | private sector | sponsor | autonomy | commercial breaks | state-run | entertainment | sponsored | licence fees | content | TV set

Television

Television was one of the most ________________ (1) inventions of the twentieth century. It is now one of our most important sources of information, opinion and ________________ (2) . In fact the average person in Britain or America ________________ (3) a quarter of his or her waking life in front of the ________________ (4). There are both ________________ (5) and privately owned broadcasting companies. State-run or public sector broadcasters are ________________ (6) by annual ________________ (7). There is generally no advertising. In Britain, for example, the BBC may not advertise or broadcast ________________ (8) programmes. However, it still has full ________________ (9) in choosing the ________________ (10) of its programmes. The ________________ (11) is financed by advertising, which is why programmes shown on these channels are frequently interrupted by ________________ (12) . Sometimes advertisers even ________________ (13) a particular programme.

From: *Words in Context*, Klett, S. 132 (adapted)

c) Combine each word on the left with one on the right to find expressions relating to media.

1. commercial *break*	fee
2. gutter ________________	coverage
3. in-depth ________________	press
4. visual ________________	material
5. newspaper ________________	break ✓
6. to be obsessed with ________________	ad
7. classified ________________	celebrities
8. licence ________________	headline

d) Find words in this topic that match these definitions or synonyms.

1. sth. you do regularly: ____________________
2. to make sth. possible: ____________________
3. overall quality or character as seen or judged by people in general: ____________________
4. one of the substances that are combined to make sth.: ____________________
5. the main information of sth.: ____________________
6. another word for effect: ____________________
7. to govern: ____________________
8. an occasion when a lot of people are asked about sth.: ____________________
9. time when one no longer works after a certain age: ____________________
10. reasonable: ____________________

e) Translate the clues below and then write the answers in the grid.

1. Zuverlässigkeit
2. Bedürfnis
3. bahnbrechend
4. Lagerung, Speicherung
5. Bratensoße
6. Geschwindigkeit
7. sachlich
8. sofortig
9. traurig
10. Ausgabe
11. Innovation

Topic 2.7 Dreams and visions

Topic vocabulary

A European issues		
notion ['nəʊʃən]	Konzept	= idea
delicate ['delɪkət]	empfindlich	= sensitive
to convey [kən'veɪ]	vermitteln	= to express
assumption [ə'sʌmpʃən]	Annahme	→ to assume
eager	eifrig	→ eagerness
admiration [ˌædmə'reɪʃən]	Bewunderung	e.g. We were filled with admiration for him.
to restore	wiederherstellen	→ restoration
B Global protests		
to be held responsible for sth.	für etw. verantwortlich gemacht werden	→ responsibility
uprising	Aufstand	→ to uprise (= aufstehen)
tentative ['tentətɪv]	vorsichtig	= careful
invincible [ɪn'vɪnsəbl]	unbesiegbar	→ invincibility
spirit	Geist	→ spiritual
a fortnight	vierzehn Tage	= two weeks
to conduct	ausführen	→ the conduct (= Benehmen, Verhalten)
dissent [dɪ'sent]	Widerspruch	= resistance
predecessor ['pri:dɪˌsesə]	Vorgänger(in)	↔ successor (= Nachfolger/in)
C Political speeches		
remark	Bemerkung	→ to remark
to appreciate [ə'pri:ʃieɪt]	schätzen, zu schätzen wissen	→ appreciation (= Schätzung, Anerkennung)
sustainable [sə'steɪnəbl]	nachhaltig, umweltgerecht	e.g. sustainable growth

prosperity [prɒs'perəti]	Wohlstand	= wealth
to soar	hochschnellen	= to rise fast
to draft	entwerfen	→ a draft (= Entwurf)
merely	lediglich	= just
D Social responsibility		
objective [əb'dʒektɪv]	Ziel	= target
loan	Darlehen, Kredit	→ to loan sth. (= jmdm etw. ausleihen)
to empower	befähigen	= to enable
expense	Kosten	= cost
nutrition [nju:'trɪʃən]	Ernährung	e.g. nutrition facts (= Nährwertangaben)
weight [weɪt]	Gewicht	→ to weigh
issue ['ɪʃu:]	Problem	= problem
fee	Gebühr	e.g. tuition fees (= Studiengebühren)
to challenge ['tʃælɪndʒ]	herausfordern	→ a challenge (= eine Herausforderung)
revenue ['revənju:]	Umsatz	= turnover
E Future living		
to derive from	sich ableiten	= to originate from
imaginary [ɪ'mædʒɪnəri]	erfunden	↔ real
current ['kʌrənt]	aktuell, gegenwärtig	→ actual (= tatsächlich)
anxiety [æŋ'zaɪəti]	Angst	= fear, worry
resistance [rɪ'zɪstəns]	Widerstand	= opposition
terrifying ['terəfaɪɪŋ]	furchterregend	= scary
to get out of hand	außer Kontrolle geraten	= to get out of control
surveillance [sɜ:'veɪləns]	Überwachung	e.g. surveillance camera
solar energy [ˌsəʊlə 'enədʒi]	Solarenergie	= solar power
breakthrough ['breɪkθru:]	Durchbruch	→ to break through

Exam practice		
understatement	Untertreibung	= a statement that makes sth. seem less important than it is
to comprise	umfassen, enthalten	= to contain
blueprint	technische Zeichnung, Plan, Entwurf	= plan, design
barely ['beəli]	kaum	= hardly
medieval [ˌmedi'i:vəl]	mittelalterlich	e.g. a medieval castle
to recognise	anerkennen	→ recognition
jigsaw ['dʒɪgsɔ:]	Puzzle	= a puzzle consisting of fragments of a picture that have to be put together correctly
evident	offensichtlich	= clear
to reside	seinen Sitz haben	= to live

Additional vocabulary

Amtszeit	term	e.g. to serve a term (= eine Amtszeit durchlaufen)
ein Gesetz verabschieden	to pass a law	↔ to veto a law
eine Gesetzesvorlage entwerfen	to draw up a bill	↔ to veto a bill
Gewaltenteilung	system of checks and balances	→ balance of power
Innenpolitik	domestic policy	↔ foreign policy
Nachfolger(in)	successor	↔ precursor [ˌpri:'kɜ:sə] (= Amtsvorgänger/in)
eine Rede halten	to deliver a speech	= to make/give a speech
schlechte Behandlung	mistreatment	→ to mistreat
Staatsbeamter, -beamtin	civil servant	= sb. who works in the civil service
seine Stimme abgeben	to cast one's vote	→ to vote (= wählen)
Stimmzettel	ballot ['bælət] paper	→ ballot box (= Wahlurne)

unparteiisch	impartial [ɪm'pɑ:ʃl]	e.g. to be politically impartial
jmdn vereidigen	to swear [sweə] sb. in	→ to swear an oath [əʊθ] (= einen Eid ablegen)
Verhältniswahlrecht	proportional [prə'pɔ:ʃnl] representation	↔ first-past-the-post system (= Mehrheitswahlrecht)
einen Vertrag ratifizieren	to ratify a treaty	→ ratification
jmdn vertreten	to represent sb.	→ representative
jmdn wählen	to elect sb.	→ election
Zusatz zur Verfassung	amendment	→ to amend a bill (= eine Gesetzesvorlage ändern)
Zustimmung	approval [ə'pru:vl]	→ to approve sth.

Exercises

a) Word family: Fill in the missing words in the table (no -ing or -ed forms). Use a dictionary and translate them into German.

Noun	**Verb**	**Adjective**
- admiration - Bewunderung		
- prosperity -		
- anxiety -	- - -	
	- to reside -	
		- imaginary -

b) Find the words in this topic that match these definitions. Then find the German meaning.

Definition	English	German
1. comment		
2. to value		
3. to carry out		
4. unconquerable		
5. to create		
6. to bring back		
7. to acknowledge		
8. obvious		
9. money you pay for a service		
10. amount of money borrowed from a bank		
11. to keep		

c) What's the word in English?

1. lediglich: ____________________
2. Ernährung: ____________________
3. Umatz: ____________________
4. Zustimmung: ____________________
5. Angst: ____________________
6. Widerstand: ____________________
7. Dünger: ____________________
8. auslösen: ____________________
9. Durchbruch: ____________________
10. kaum: ____________________
11. Solarenergie: ____________________

d) Translate the clues below and then write the answers in the grid.

1. hochschnellen
2. mittelalterlich
3. unparteiisch
4. vierzehn Tage
5. Vorgänger
6. Zusatz zur Verfassung
7. Bedrohung
8. Konzept
9. Nachfolger
10. Widerspruch
11. Bewunderung

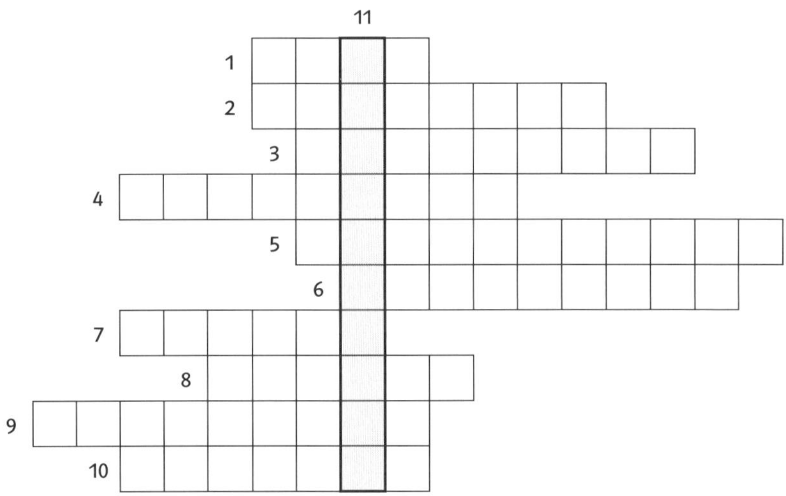

Topic 2.8 Cross-cultural issues

Topic vocabulary

Getting started		
superstition [ˌsu:pə'stɪʃən]	Aberglaube	→ superstitious
inferior [ɪn'fɪəriə]	minderwertig	→ inferiority
fringe [frɪndʒ]	Rand	= edge
to mask [mɑ:sk]	verbergen	= to hide sth.
A Racial stereotypes		
to spot	entdecken	= to discover
allegedly [ə'ledʒɪdli]	angeblich	= supposedly
to assault [ə'sɔ:lt]	angreifen	= to attack
offender	Straftäter(in)	→ offence (= Straftat)
biased ['baɪəst]	voreingenommen	→ bias (= Vorurteil)
reluctant [rɪ'lʌktənt]	widerwillig, widerstrebend	→ reluctance (= Unwille, Unlust)
juvenile ['dʒu:vənaɪl]	Jugend-	e.g. juvenile delinquency [dɪ'lɪŋkwənsi] (= Jugendkriminalität)
B National identity		
issue ['ɪʃu:]	Thema	= topic
mosque [mɒsk]	Moschee	= Islamic place of worship
despite	trotz	= in spite of
fragile ['frædʒaɪl]	zerbrechlich, schwach	→ fragility
appeal	Anreiz	= attraction
C Cross-cultural attitudes		
to disguise [dɪs'gaɪz] oneself	sich verkleiden	= to take on a different appearance
property ['prɒpəti]	Eigentum	= sth. you own

to pursue sb. [pə'sju:]	jmdn bedrängen, jagen	→ pursuit (= Jagd, Streben)
to disobey [ˌdɪsə'beɪ]	nicht gehorchen	↔ to obey
engaged [ɪn'geɪdʒd]	verlobt	→ engagement ring (= Verlobungsring)
heir [eə]	der Erbe/die Erbin	→ inheritance (= das Erbe)
stain [steɪn]	Fleck	→ to stain (= etw. verschmutzen)
D Immigration		
to keep track of sth.	über etw. Aufzeichnungen machen	= to keep record of sth.
resident	Bewohner(in)	= inhabitant
commitment [kə'mɪtmənt]	Bindung, Engagement	→ to be committed (= engagiert sein)
fortunate ['fɔ:tʃənət]	glücklich	= lucky
to provide for	sorgen für, versorgen	= to look after
E Patriotism		
to found	gründen	→ foundation
punishment	Strafe, Bestrafung	→ to punish
to gather ['gæðə]	zusammenkommen	= to get together
to highlight	hervorheben	= to stress
to witness	beobachten	→ a witness (= Zeuge)
to leap	springen	= to jump
to deny	abstreiten	→ denial (= Bestreiten, Leugnen)
Exam practice		
perception [pə'sepʃən]	Wahrnehmung, Vorstellung	→ to perceive (= wahrnehmen, bemerken)
to dilute [daɪ'lu:t]	verdünnen, schwächen	→ dilution (= Abschwächung, Verwässerung)
flawed [flɔ:d]	fehlerhaft	→ flaw (= Fehler)
crucial ['kru:ʃəl]	entscheidend	= very important

Additional vocabulary

annehmen	to accept	↔ to refuse
(sich) anpassen	to assimilate [ə'sɪmɪleɪt]	→ assimilation
Argwohn	suspicion [sə'spɪʃən]	↔ trust
Asylbewerber(in)	asylum [ə'saɪləm] seeker	→ to seek asylum
Durchschnitts-, etabliert	mainstream	→ mainstream trend (= genereller Trend)
Einwanderung	immigration	↔ emigration
Einwanderungspolitik	immigration policy	e.g. a restrictive immigration policy
Flüchtling	refugee [ˌrefjʊ'dʒiː]	= sb. who flees her/his country because of persecution
fördern	to promote	= to support
Groll, Vorbehalte	resentment	→ to resent sb. (= jmdm grollen)
Hass	hatred	e.g. racial hatred against ethnic minorities
integrieren	to integrate	→ integration
Intoleranz gegenüber anderen Rassen	racial intolerance	→ intolerant
Menschenhandel	human trafficking ['træfɪkɪŋ]	→ drug trafficking
Menschenrechte	human rights	e.g. to violate human rights
Minderheit	minority [maɪ'nɒrəti]	↔ majority
Opfer	victim	= sb. who suffers because of a bad situation
Rassismus	racism	→ racist
Schikane	harassment ['hærəsmənt]	→ to harass
Schleier	veil [veɪl]	= sth. that is worn by women to cover their faces
Sitte, Brauch	custom	e.g. to retain an old custom
Sozialausgaben	welfare expenses	→ to be on welfare
Spannung	tension	e.g. to stir racial tensions
Staatsbürger(in)	citizen	→ citizenship

Sündenbock	scapegoat	= sb. who is blamed for sth.
Unternehmergeist	entrepreneurial [ˌɒntrəprəˈnɜːrɪəl] spirit	→ entrepreneur (= Unternehmer/in)
unterscheiden	to distinguish [dɪˈstɪŋgwɪʃ]	= to differentiate
unzureichend	inadequate [ɪˈnædɪkwət]	↔ adequate
Vergeltung	retaliation [rɪˌtælɪˈeɪʃn]	e.g. in retaliation (= zur Vergeltung)
etw. verletzen	to violate	→ violation
Vorurteile gegenüber anderen Rassen	racial prejudice [ˈpredʒədɪs]	→ prejudiced (= voreingenommen)
Zu- und Abwanderung	migration	→ to migrate

Exercises

a) Word family: Fill in the missing words in the table (no -ing or -ed forms). Use a dictionary and translate them into German.

Noun	Verb	Adjective
	– to accept – annehmen	
– offence/offender –		
– diversity –		
	– to promote –	– – –

b) Complete the text with the words from below.

mainstream | teaching assistant | wear | debate | language | to take of | veil | race relations | stir | tolerant | case | customs | remarks | multiculturalism | point out | suspended | refused | doubts | terrorism | leaders

In multicultural Britain a debate about the Muslim veil

Should Muslim women in Britain ________________ (1) a full-face veil? Does covering the face cause separation and could it even be bad for ____________________________ (2)? These are the questions Britons are discussing after _______________ (3) by a British politician. He said that he asks veiled Muslim women to take of their ________________ (4) as he cannot have a real "face-to-face" conversation with a person if all he can see is their eyes.

The debate on the veil became more heated with the ________________ (5) of Aishah Azmi. The young woman wore the full veil while working as a ____________________________ (6) at a school in Dewsburry, West Yorkshire. She helped ethnic minority children whose first ________________ (7) was not English. The school asked her ________________ (8) her veil in the classroom as it was important for the children to see their teacher's lips when she spoke. However Ms Azmi ________________ (9) to move her veil and was ____________ (10) from her job.

The ________________ (11) is more than just about style of dress or the interpretation of religion: it is about ____________________________ (12) and about how far non-Christian immigrants can be expected to integrate. Up until now, Britain has accepted different ________________ (13) and traditions of its immigrants, but since the increase of ________________ (14), in particular attacks by British Muslims on London transport, there have been ________________ (15) about multiculturalism, and demands for better integration. Muslims must become part of ____________________________ (16) British society to ensure that they do not become radicalised, say some.

Others ________________ (17) criticism of different customs – like wearing a veil – can lead to racism. Both Muslim and non-Muslim ________________ (18) agree that a debate on issues like the veil is important, but it is just as important that it is carried on in a ________________ (19) manner that does not ________________ (20) racial hatred.

From: *Read On*, www.sprachzeitungen.de (adapted)

c) Translate the clues below and then write the answers in the grid.

1. Moschee
2. Bewohner
3. Groll, Vorbehalt
4. Sitte, Brauch
5. glücklich
6. Opfer
7. Hass
8. gehorchen
9. Minderheit

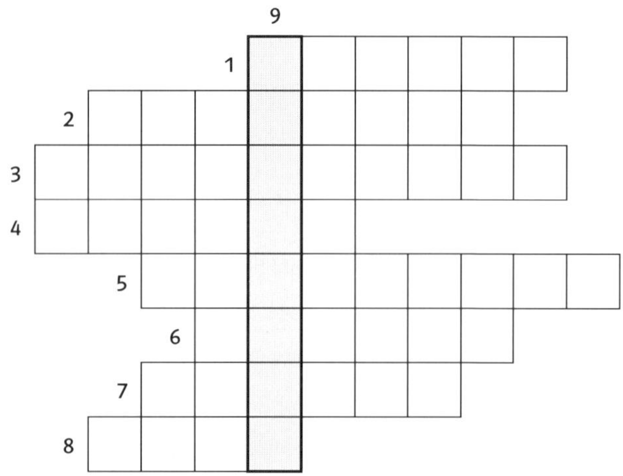

d) Complete the word web with words or phrases from below.

- ethnic minorities
- inadequate
- unskilled immigrants
- different food
- society (2x)
- discrimination
- economy (2x)
- entrepreneurial spirit
- skilled workers
- labour
- ageing society
- lower wages
- tensions
- welfare expenses
- business contacts
- scapegoats

Immigration

benefits for ______________

- ______________
- new ideas and languages
- reduce the effects of an ______________ (often young and a lot of children)

benefits for the ______________

- cheap ______________
- innovative ideas and ______________
- ______________ to other countries
- ______________ in needed sectors

disadvantages for ______________

- often ______________ for all kinds of problems
- racial ______________
- ______________ against ______________
- ______________ for unskilled workers

disadvantages for the ______________

- often ______________ language skills
- almost no jobs for ______________
- high ______________

Topic 2.9 The global challenge

Topic vocabulary

Getting started		
debt [det]	Schulden	→ debt relief (= Schuldenerlass)
sweatshop	Ausbeutungsbetrieb	= a factory where workers are exploited
A Discovering globalisation		
roughly ['rʌfli]	ungefähr	= about, approximately
to collaborate [kə'læbəreɪt]	zusammenarbeiten	= to work together
primarily [praɪ'merəli]	hauptsächlich	= mainly
B A fair world?		
to make a living	den Lebensunterhalt verdienen	= to earn money
to survive	überleben	→ survival
to encourage [ɪn'kʌrɪdʒ]	ermutigen	↔ to discourage
reward	Belohnung	→ to reward
to respond	reagieren	= to react
approach	Herangehensweise	= a way of dealing with sth.
conscience ['kɒnʃəns]	Gewissen	= sense of what is right or wrong
C Global players		
advantage	Vorteil	= benefit
loss [lɒs]	Verlust	→ to lose
economic cycle	Konjunktur	= the development of an economy
shares	Aktien	= stocks
currency ['kʌrənsi]	Währung	= the money of a country
to turn over	umsetzen	→ turnover (= Umsatz)

byproduct	Nebenprodukt	= sth. which is produced during the production process of sth. else
to exceed [ɪk'si:d]	übersteigen	= to surpass
D Corporate power		
to abolish	abschaffen	→ abolition
to shift	wechseln	= to move
relief [rɪ'li:f]	Erleichterung	→ to relieve
cute [kju:t]	süß	= sweet
hypocritical [ˌhɪpəʊ'krɪtɪkəl]	heuchlerisch	→ hypocrisy (= Heuchelei)
E Water poverty		
lack	Mangel	→ to lack
sanitation [ˌsænɪ'teɪʃən]	Abwassersystem, sanitäre Anlagen	e.g. toilet, shower
due to	wegen	= because of
to exacerbate [ɪg'zæsəbeɪt]	verschlimmern	↔ to improve
foundation [faʊn'deɪʃən]	Gründung, Fundament	→ to found
asset	Vermögen, Wirtschaftsgut	= resource
to foster	fördern, pflegen	e.g. a foster family (= Pflegefamilie)
Spot on language		
to incline	neigen	→ inclination (= Neigung)
vice versa [ˌvaɪsi'vɜ:sə]	umgekehrt	= the other way round
Exam practice		
blessing ['blesɪŋ]	Segen	↔ curse (= Fluch)
prospect ['prɒspekt]	Aussicht	e.g. good business prospects
downturn	Abschwung	↔ upturn
roots [ru:ts]	Wurzeln	= origin
failure ['feɪljə]	Versagen	→ to fail
neglect [nɪ'glekt]	Nichtbeachtung	→ to neglect

to gain	gewinnen	= to profit
to strive [straɪv]	streben nach	= to try hard to achieve sth.
inevitable [ɪ'nevɪtəbl]	unvermeidlich	= unavoidable

Additional vocabulary

das Allernotwendigste	essentials [ɪ'senʃəlz]	e.g. Food, water, clothing and shelter are essentials.
Anpassungsfähigkeit	adaptability [əˌdæptə'bɪləti]	= ability to change
Armut	poverty	↔ wealth
aushandeln	to negotiate [nɪ'gəʊʃɪˌeɪt]	e.g. to negotiate a trade agreement
Bedrohung	threat [θret]	→ to threaten
zu etw. beitragen	to contribute to sth.	→ contribution
Fortschritt	advancement	e.g. technological advancement
Freigabe	liberalisation [ˌlɪbərəlaɪ'zeɪʃən]	= removal of restrictions
gerechte Handels-bedingungen	fair trading conditions	→ fair trade
Gewinn	profit	→ profitable
Globalisierung	globalisation	e.g. economic globalisation
Handel	trade	e.g. trade fair (= Handelsmesse)
Hilfe, Entwicklungshilfe	aid	= financial help
Investition	investment	→ to invest in sth.
Kapitalmarkt	capital market	e.g. to borrow money from the capital market
Kaufkraft	purchasing ['pɜ:tʃəsɪŋ] power	e.g. increased purchasing power
eine Kluft überbrücken	to bridge a gap	e.g. to bridge a gap between the poor and the rich
kontrovers, strittig	controversial	→ controversy
auf Kosten von etw./jmdm gehen	to be at the expense of sth./sb.	→ expenses (= Ausgaben)

Lebenserwartung	life expectancy [ɪk'spektənsɪ]	e.g. Life expectancy increased during the last century.
Lebensstandard	living standard	e.g. to raise living standards
an etw. leiden	to suffer from sth.	e.g. to suffer from malnutrition (= Unterernährung)
Quote	quota ['kwəʊtə]	e.g. to set a quota
einen Streit beilegen	to settle a dispute	e.g. The WTO tries to settle trade disputes.
subventioniert	subsidized	→ subsidy
Ungleichheit	inequality	↔ equality
etw. verlegen	to relocate sth.	e.g. to relocate a factory to a country with cheap labour
Voraussetzung	precondition	= requirement
Wirtschaft	economy	→ economic (= wirtschaftlich) → economical (= sparsam)
Zugang zu etw. haben	to have access to sth.	e.g. to have access to sanitation (= Sanitäreinrichtungen)
jmdm zugutekommen	to benefit sb.	→ to benefit from sth. (= von etw. profitieren)
Zusammenschluss	merger ['mɜːdʒə]	→ to merge

Exercises

a) What's the word in English?

1. Erleichterung: ______________
2. süß: ______________
3. Hilfe, Entwicklungshilfe: ______________
4. Bedrohung: ______________
5. unvermeidlich: ______________
6. Vermögen: ______________
7. verschlimmern: ______________
8. Gründung, Fundament: ______________
9. Zusammenschluss: ______________
10. neigen: ______________
11. subventioniert: ______________
12. Voraussetzung: ______________

b) Complete the text with the words from below.

immigration | multinational companies | pollution | ethnic tensions | humanity | slogan | understanding | gap | fear | opportunities | conflicts | expects | prosperity | foreign | globalisation | predict | human rights | universal values | governments (2x) | spread of freedom | mass media | stability

Globalisation

The developing countries hope that ________________ (1) will bring them work and ________________ (2), whereas the industrial world ________________ (3) increased business opportunities through international trade. In addition, it is hoped that the ________________ (4), democracy and ________________ (5) will reduce the number of wars and other ________________ (6) worldwide. The increasing ________________ (7) for exchange on a personal level may lead to a greater ________________ (8) among peoples around the world, which could bring about a peaceful, borderless world of shared ________________ (9), general economic prosperity and ecological ________________ (10). In the developing countries many people ________________ (11) an increasing dependence on ________________ (12) support, investment and credit. Some see danger in increasingly corrupt ________________ (13), negative cultural influences and even manipulation through the ________________ (14). In the industrial world experts ________________ (15) both the erosion of national cultures in Europe and massive illegal ________________ (16). The increasing power of ________________ (17) is problematic because they can often no longer be controlled by legal means such as elected ________________ (18). For ________________ (19) as a whole there is the fear that largely uncontrolled economic activity will result in inequality and regional and ________________ (20), as well as in ________________ (21). The "survival of the fittest" could become the ________________ (22) of an inhumane, competitive global world. The so-called Westernisation of the world is predicted to widen the ________________ (23) between the rich and the poor.

c) Word family: Fill in the missing words in the table (no -ing or -ed forms). Use a dictionary and translate them into German.

Noun	Verb	Adjective
	– to respond – reagieren	
– adaptability –		
– liberalisation –		
– prospect –	– – –	
		– global –

d) Translate the clues below and then write the answers in the grid.

1. Aktien
2. Abschwung
3. Segen
4. Versagen
5. Schulden
6. Aussicht
7. abschaffen
8. verlegen
9. Herangehensweise
10. Ausbeutungsbetrieb

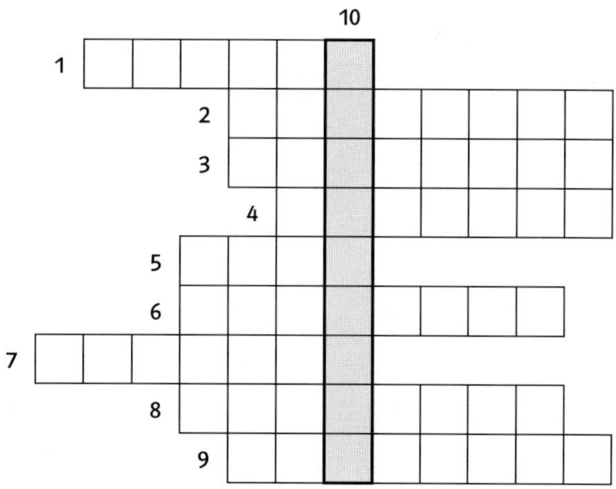

e) Complete the word web with words or phrases from below.

- choosing best places for certain tasks
- companies make more and more profits
- creation of new jobs
- fast transportation worldwide
- information and communication technology
- hopes
- new demand through innovation
- only the rich benefit
- preconditions
- social responsibility of companies

company aspects

- ____________________
- mobility of goods/capital/products
- ____________________

[____________________]

- ____________________
- rising standard of living
- ____________________

Globalisation

fears

- ____________________
- loss of work places
- ____________________

[____________________]

- ____________________
- ____________________
- free trade

Topic 2.10 Marketing and media

Topic vocabulary

A The influence of advertising		
behaviour [bɪ'heɪvjə]	Verhalten	e.g. behaviour pattern (= Verhaltensmuster)
desirable [dɪ'zaɪərəbl]	wünschenswert	= preferable
brand	Marke	e.g. Levis is a famous American brand.
embarrassment [ɪm'bærəsmənt]	Peinlichkeit	→ to embarrass (= in Verlegenheit bringen)
anxiety [æŋ'zaɪəti]	Angst	→ anxious
unique [ju:'ni:k]	einzigartig	→ uniqueness
to mature [mə'tjʊə]	reifen	→ maturity
at one's disposal	zur Verfügung	= to have sth. available to you
subtle ['sʌtl]	dezent	= understated
to combat	bekämpfen	→ combat
to coincide [ˌkəʊɪn'saɪd]	übereinstimmen	→ coincidence (= Zufälligkeit)
B New media and infotainment		
rival	Wettbewerber(in)	= competitor
current ['kʌrənt]	aktuell	e.g. current affairs (= aktuelle Nachrichten)
affiliation [əˌfɪli'eɪʃn]	Verbindung	→ to affiliate (= sich anschließen)
encouragement	Ermutigung	→ to encourage
separation	Trennung	= division
C Consumer protection		
to launch [lɔ:nʃ]	auf den Markt bringen	e.g. product launch
advocate ['ædvəkət]	Befürworter(in)	= supporter

proposal	Vorschlag	→ to propose
to exploit	ausbeuten	= to take unfair advantage of
to maintain [meɪn'teɪn]	behaupten	= to claim
consistent with	übereinstimmend mit	= in agreement with
to prevent	verhindern	= to stop
D Food consumption: We are what we eat		
to pose	darstellen	e.g. to pose a problem (= ein Problem aufwerfen)
awkward ['ɔ:kwəd]	seltsam	= strange
to tackle	bewältigen	= to successfully deal with sth.
pertinent ['pɜ:tɪnənt]	relevant	= relevant
poultry ['pəʊltrɪ]	Geflügel	= meat from birds such as chickens
to retain	behalten	= to keep
E The art world		
offshore	vor der Küste	= situated at sea some distance from the shore
to struggle	kämpfen	→ the struggle
to emerge [ɪ'mɜ:dʒ]	herauskommen, aufkommen	→ emergence (= das Aufkommen)
staff [stɑ:f]	Personal	= employees
exhibition	Ausstellung	→ to exhibit
Exam practice		
union ['ju:njən]	Gewerkschaft	→ to unionise (= sich gewerkschaftlich organisieren)
naughty ['nɔ:ti]	unanständig	= behaving badly
to cover	abdecken, hier: ausstrahlen	→ coverage (= Abdeckung, Berichterstattung)

Additional vocabulary

(Werbe-)Anzeige	advertisement [əd'vɜ:tɪsmənt]	→ to advertise
anzeigen, zur Schau stellen	to display	→ a display
Bequemlichkeit	convenience [kən'vi:nɪəns]	→ convenient
Besitz	possession	= belongings, property
Botschaft	message	e.g. to get the message
Dienstleistung	service	= help that you give to sb.
dringende Bitte, Anziehungskraft	appeal	→ to appeal
Einkaufssüchtige(r)	shopaholic	= sb. who is addicted to shopping
erreichen, bewerkstelligen	to accomplish	→ an accomplishment
ersetzen	to substitute	= to replace
Fernsehwerbung, Werbespot	commercial [kə'mɜ:ʃəl]	e.g. The new car commercial is very funny.
identifizieren	to identify	→ identification
kaufen	to purchase	= to buy
Konsum, Verbrauch	consumption	→ consumer, to consume
Kosmetikprodukte	beauty products	= cosmetics
Marke	brand	e.g. brand loyalty
rechtzeitig	in due course	= in time, punctual
Schnäppchen	bargain	= a good deal
Sonderangebot	special offer	= sth. that can be bought at a reduced price
spontane(r) Käufer(in)	impulse buyer ['ɪmpʌls ˌbaɪə]	= sb. who buys things without thinking too much about it
stark herabgesetzt	cut-price	= a very low price
Status steigernd	status-enhancing	e.g. A fancy car is status-enhancing.
süchtig nach etw.	addicted to sth.	→ addiction
tendieren, neigen	to tend	e.g. She tends to interrupt other people.
überreden	to persuade [pə'sweɪd]	→ to convince

Umfrage	survey	→ to survey
in Verbindung bringen	to associate [ə'səʊʃɪət]	→ association
weitverbreitet	widespread	= being used in many different situations
Werbespruch	slogan	= a phrase that is easy to remember

Exercises

a) Word family: Fill in the missing words in the table (no -ing or -ed forms). Use a dictionary and translate them into German.

Noun	Verb	Adjective
	– to exploit – ausbeuten	
		– sustainable –
		– desirable –

b) What's the word in English?

1. Peinlichkeit: ______________________
2. etw. behaupten: ______________________
3. Vorschlag: ______________________
4. Marke: ______________________
5. Verbindung: ______________________
6. Ermutigung: ______________________
7. seltsam: ______________________
8. Geflügel: ______________________
9. Verhalten: ______________________
10. bewältigen: ______________________
11. Anziehungskraft: ______________________
12. überreden: ______________________

c) Complete the text with the verbs from below. Two verbs don't fit.

accomplished | are | buy | seen | summarizes | stay
compare | feel | go | shop | involves | tend
have to | help | matter | pay | think (2x) | make

Shop till you drop

Leading experts on brain research __________ (1) that women __________ (2) to live longer than men because they __________ (3) more. It doesn't __________ (4) if you __________ (5) clothes or groceries, shopping __________ (6) what's good for the brain. Being physically active, challenging the brain and keeping a positive self-image __________ (7) three major elements that __________ (8) the brain to function in a better way.

"For the last time, stop saving me money!"

When women __________ (9) shopping they often __________ (10) walk around a lot with heavy bags. They also have to __________ (11) prices and then __________ (12) decisions what to buy. Afterwards they __________ (13) good about themselves because they __________ (14) that they have __________ (15) something. Men, on the other hand, often __________ (16) at home in front of the TV which __________ (17) none of the above mentioned elements.

d) Find words in this topics that match these definitions.

1. to become older and more developed: __________
2. a place where art or products are displayed: __________
3. sth. bought cheaply or for less than its usual price: __________
4. to be in agreement with: __________
5. one of a kind: __________
6. effect: __________

7. a feeling of fear or worry about sth. : ______________________

8. the people who work for a company: ______________________

9. to have problems with: ______________________

e) Complete the text with the words from below. Two words don't fit.

associated	happy	shopaholics	widespread	necessary	
basic needs	lacking	identify	status-enhancing	unnecessary	
display	happiness	opponents	tendency	term	phenomenon

Consumerism

Consumerism is a ______________ (1) used to describe the effects of equating personal ______________________ (2) with purchasing material possessions and consumption. Although consumerism is commonly ________________ (3) with the Western world, it is multi-cultural and non-geographical. Consumerism, as in people purchasing goods or consuming materials in excess of their ______________________ (4), is as old as the first civilizations.

While consumerism is not a new ____________________ (5), it has only become ______________________ (6) over the 20th century and particularly in recent decades. In many critical contexts, consumerism is used to describe the ____________________ (7) of people to ____________________ (8) strongly with products or services they consume, especially those with commercial brand names and obvious ______________________ (9) appeal, e.g. an expensive automobile. Impulse buyers who cannot resist spending money are commonly termed ____________________ (10). ______________________ (11) of consumerism argue that many luxuries and ______________________ (12) consumer products are social signals that allow people to identify like-minded individuals through consumption and ______________ (13) of similar products. Some believe that relationships with a product or brand name are substitutes for the healthy human relationships ______________________ (14) in modern societies.

From: *Wikipedia* (adapted)

Key to the exercises

1.1 Being young today

a)

Noun	**Verb**	**Adjective**
– validation – Bestätigung, Gültigkeit	– to validate – bestätigen	– valid – gültig
– vulnerability – Verletzbarkeit	– – –	– vulnerable – verletzlich
– acquisition – Erwerb	– to acquire – erwerben	– – –
– success – Erfolg	– to succeed – Erfolg haben	– successful – erfolgreich
– reliability – Zuverlässigkeit	– to rely on sb. – sich auf jmdn verlassen	– reliable – zuverlässig

b) 1. provide – 2. give – 3. may seem – 4. create – 5. are doing – 6. offer – 7. Take – 8. can design – 9. keep – 10. organise – 11. provides – 12. is – 13. describes – 14. can be – 15. allow – 16. wanders – 17. interact

c) 1. to settle into – 2. to ban – 3. to intervene – 4. to blush – 5. exposure to – 6. to graduate – 7. dedicated – 8. adolescent – 9. evidence – 10. duty – 11. entitlement – 12. to gossip – 13. to facilitate – 14. to tease sb.

d) 1. superficial – 2. acquire – 3. self-esteem – 4. admit – 5. release – 6. truancy – 7. achieve – 8. obesity – 9. patience

1.2 Personal identities and social relationships

a)

Noun	**Verb**	**Adjective**
- depth - Tiefe	- to deepen - vertiefen	- deep - tief
- accumulation - Anhäufung, Ansammlung	- to accumulate - anhäufen, sich ansammeln	- accumulative - wachsend
- exhaust - Abgas, Abdampf	- to exhaust - ausbeuten, erschöpfen	- exhaustive - erschöpfend, umfassend
- abuse - Missbrauch	- to abuse - missbrauchen	- abusive - missbräuchlich
- ease - Erleichterung	- to ease - erleichtern	- easy - leicht

b) 1. affection – 2. to improve – 3. prejudice – 4. acquaintance – 5. counsellor – 6. to have a row with so. – 7. to rebel – 8. gender – 9. significance – 10. to decline

c)

household chore	Hausarbeit
bridal bouquet	Brautstrauß
to foster a child	ein Kind in Pflege nehmen
to lose one's temper	die Beherrschung verlieren
sibling rivalry	Rivalität unter Geschwistern
to file for divorce	die Scheidung einreichen
contemporary art	zeitgenössische Kunst
marital problem	Eheproblem
behavioral pattern	Verhaltensmuster
peer group	Alterskohorte

d) 1. peer – 2. to release – 3. to row – 4. unfortunate – 5. improvement – 6. to reveal

e) Across: 1. label – 4. compassion – 6. appreciate – 8. puberty – 10. prejudice – 11. affection – 12. distribution – 14. coincidence – 15. burden – 16. shift
Down: 2. abuse – 3. significance – 5. bully – 7. temporary – 9. mood – 13. depth

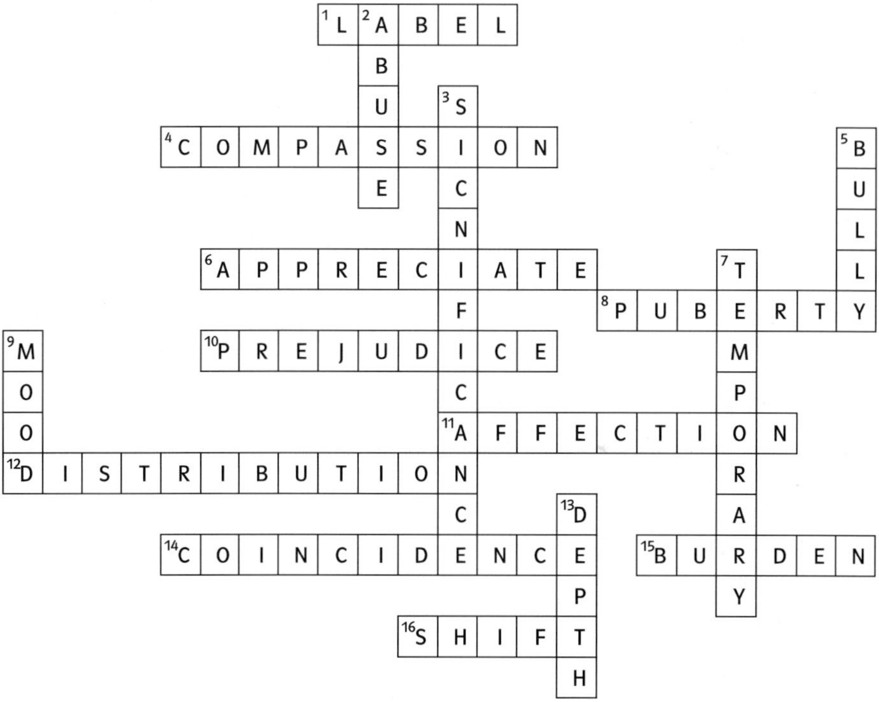

1.3 Progress, sustainability and responsibility

a) 1. to subsidise, subventionieren – 2. to replicate, kopieren – 3. to take for granted, etw. als selbstverständlich hinnehmen – 4. drought, Dürre – 5. self-esteem, Selbstwertgefühl – 6. venue, Veranstaltungsort – 7. to oppose, ablehnen, bekämpfen – 8. to deplete, sich verringern – 9. tide, Gezeiten – 10. pollutant, Schadstoff – 11. abundant, reichlich – 12. natural resources, Bodenschätze – 13. overhaul, Überarbeitung – 14. combustion, Verbrennung – 15. reckless, rücksichtslos

b) 1. hazardous – 2. drought – 3. habitat – 4. grid – 5. ancient – 6. binding – 7. scale – 8. glacier – 9. vapour – 10. yield – 11. deliberate – 12. evidence

c) Energy

renewable
- type
  - solar
  - **wind**
  - **geothermal**
  - **hydroelectric**
  - **tidal**
- advantages
  - **non-depleting**
  - **no CO_2-emissions**
- disadvantages
  - often no constant flow of energy
  - **still expensive**

nuclear
- advantages
  - **cheap**
  - **no CO_2-emissions**
- disadvantages
  - waste problem
  - **dangerous**

fossil
- type
  - oil
  - **coal**
  - **natural gas**
- advantages
  - **comparably cheap**
- disadvantages
  - **depleting**
  - **CO_2-emissions**
  - **pollution**

d) 1. is – 2. face – 3. affect – 4. are – 5. will leave – 6. will experience – 7. will suffer – 8. do not have – 9. is needed – 10. is made worse – 11. is often polluted – 12. is (*haven't* and *affects* don't fit)

1.4 Britain and the United States

a) 1. desertification – 2. to preserve – 3. persecution – 4. arid – 5. population – 6. commuter – 7. famine – 8. to require sth. – 9. to hijack

b) 1. arid – 2. volunteer – 3. poverty – 4. vacant – 5. pollution – 6. rural

c) 1. call – 2. has – 3. think – 4. are – 5. printed – 6. can be – 7. says – 8. is made up – 9. does not include – 10. write – 11. mean – 12. be avoided – 13. say – 14. mean – 15. is – 16. refer to – 17. is – 18. want – 19. must call – 20. is

d)

Noun	Verb	Adjective
- prediction - Vorhersage	- to predict - vorhersagen	- predictable - vorhersagbar
- response - Antwort	- to respond - antworten	- responsive - reaktionsfähig, reagierend
- volunteer - Freiwillige(r)	- to volunteer - sich freiwillig melden	- voluntary - freiwillig
- population - Bevölkerung	- to populate - bevölkern	- populous - bevölkerungsreich

e) 1. extent – 2. sovereignty – 3. to commute –4. debris –5. doubtful – 6. rural – 7. vacant

f) 1. habitat – 2. harvest – 3. pesticide – 4. donation – 5. eviction – 6. concrete

1.5 Private and professional communication

a)

Noun	Verb	Adjective
- substitute - Ersatz	- to substitute - ersetzen	- substitutable - ersetzbar
- elaboration - Vervollkommnung, Ausarbeitung	- to elaborate - sorgfältig ausarbeiten	- elaborate - kompliziert
- obsession - Besessenheit, Manie	- to obsess sb. - jmdn verfolgen	- obsessed, obsessive - besessen, zwanghaft
- intention - Absicht	- to intend - beabsichtigen	- intentional - absichtlich
- progress - Fortschritt	- to progress - fortschreiten	- progressive - fortschrittlich

b) 1. literate – 2. to remain – 3. to found – 4. selfish – 5. invoice – 6. majority – 7. to enhance – 8. to appreciate – 9. to acknowledge – 10. flaw – 11. to emerge – 12. warehouse

c) 1. to found – 2. to intend – 3. to maintain – 4. substantial – 5. prospect – 6. enquiry – 7. intention – 8. actual – 9. complicated – 10. order

d) **Across:** 3. substitute – 5. according to – 8. VAT – 9. sample – 12. emergence – 13. recommend – 15. substantial
Down: 1. discount – 2. spouse – 4. terms – 6. involve – 7. fair – 10. demand – 11. bank transfer – 14. range – 16. supply

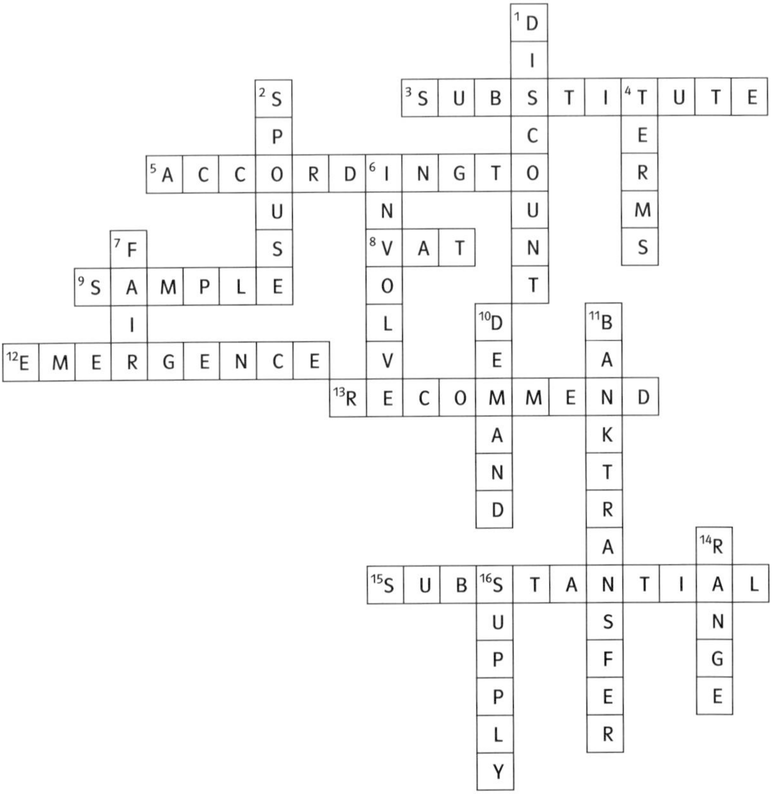

2.1 The English language in use

a)

Noun	Verb	Adjective
- adviser, advice - Ratgeber, Rat	- to advise - raten	- advisable - ratsam
- perception - Wahrnehmung	- to perceive - wahrnehmen	- perceivable - wahrnehmbar
- predominance - Vorherrschaft	- to predominate - vorherrschen	- predominant - vorherrschend
- deceit - Betrug	- to deceive sb. - jmdn betrügen	- deceitful - betrügerisch
- access - Zugang	- to access - eintreten	- accessible - zugänglich
- hesitation - Zögern	- to hesitate - zögern	- hesitant - zögerlich
- negotiation - Verhandlung	- to negotiate - verhandeln	- negotiable - aushandelbar
- comprehension - Verständnis	- to comprehend - verstehen	- comprehensible - verständlich

b) 1. ingredients – 2. plot – 3. although – 4. anticipation – 5. tension – 6. well-chosen – 7. action – 8. fitting atmosphere – 9. Believable – 10. round – 11. reasons – 12. identify – 13. strong opening – 14. immediately – 15. devices – 16. employ
(*tragedy* and *manipulation* do not fit!)

c) 1. clumsy – 2. to expose – 3. to impose – 4. to censor – 5. venture – 6. unanimous – 7. ambition – 8. casualty – 9. requirement – 10. application – 11. unprecedented

d) 1. bold – 2. tie – 3. emphasis – 4. to struggle – 5. compulsory – 6. native – 7. periodical – 8. appeal – 9. advance – 10. to counter – 11. casualty – 12. riot

e) 1. curriculum – 2. lingua franca – 3. censor – 4. blog – 5. secure – 6. feature – 7. ingredient – 8. setting – 9. language

2.2 The United States – then and now

a)

to withdraw troops	Truppen zurückziehen
to depreciate a machine	eine Maschine abschreiben
to revitalize a neighbourhood	eine Gegend wiederbeleben
to negotiate a contract	einen Vertrag verhandeln
to expel a student	einen Schüler von der Schule weisen
to liberate a captive	einen Gefangenen befreien
to commute to work	zur Arbeit pendeln
to betray a friend	einen Freund betrügen
to marginalize minorities	Minderheiten an den Rand drängen
to bear arms	Waffen tragen

b)

Noun	Verb	Adjective
– attainment – Erlangung, Erreichung	– to attain – erreichen	– attainable – erreichbar
– reliability – Zuverlässigkeit	– to rely on – sich verlassen auf	– reliable – zuverlässig
– persistence – Beharren, Ausdauer	– to persist – bestehen, beharren	– persistent – beharrlich, ausdauernd
– dependence – Abhängigkeit	– to depend on – abhängig sein von	– dependent – abhängig
– influence – Einfluss	– to influence – beeinflussen	– influential – einflussreich

c) 1. primary – 2. applicant – 3. inauguration – 4. to dishonor – 5. settler – 6. vacant – 7. to foreclose – 8. to propose to sb. – 9. allusion – 10. self-evident – 11. segregation – 12. to ratify – 13. subprime mortgage crisis – 14. to intervene – 15. burden – 16. disparity

d) Across: 3. concise – 4. slave – 6. dishonor – 8. sore – 9. vacant – 10. conceive – 14. ingrained – 15. disarmament – 16. treaty
Down: 1. secular – 2. invasion – 5. foreclose – 7. humiliation – 11. persist – 12. advise – 13. gloomy

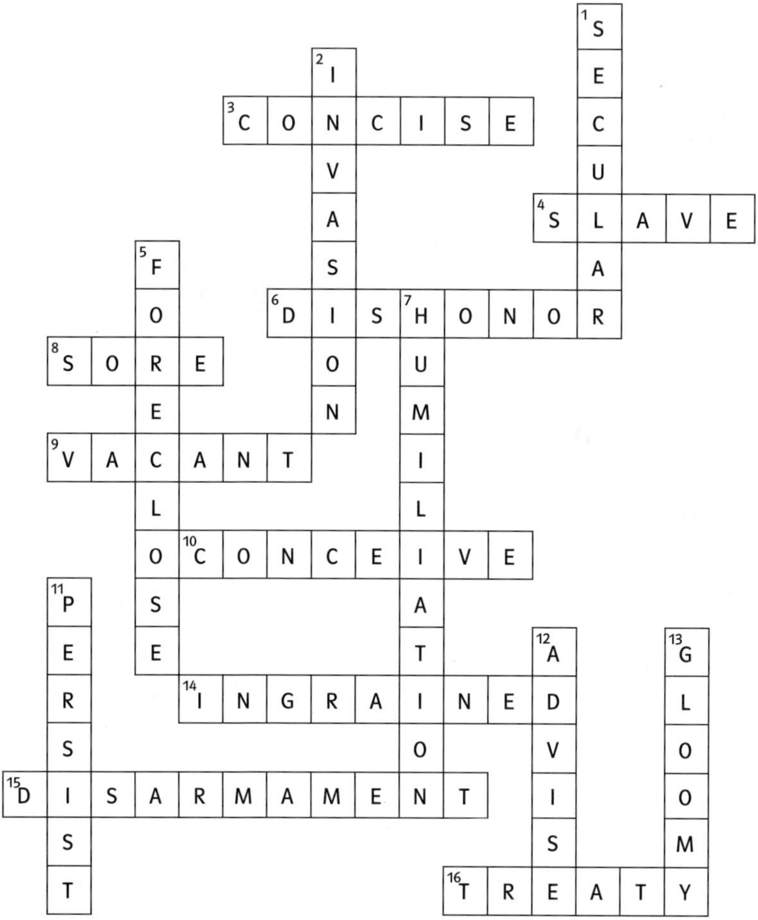

2.3 The United Kingdom – then and now

a)

– adjustment – Anpassung	– to adjust – anpassen	– adjustable – anpassbar
– government – Regierung	– to govern – leiten, regieren	– governmental – Regierungs-
– urge – Drang, Trieb	– to urge – drängen	– urgent – dringend
– oppression – Unterdrückung	– to oppress – unterdrücken	– oppressive – unterdrückend
– colony – Kolonie	– to colonize – ein Land besiedeln	– colonial – kolonial

b) 1. CCTV – 2. foremost – 3. prejudice – 4. judiciary – 5. House of Lords – 6. head of state – 7. legislative period – 8. encouragement – 9. first-past-the-post system – 10. ingrained – 11. reign – 12. proponent

c) 1. subject – 2. civil servant – 3. feasible – 4. evident – 5. to reinforce – 6. to conquer – 7. GDP – 8. capable – 9. to oppose – 10. affection – 11. to rely on – 12. to acknowledge

d) 1. Prime Minister – 2. to become – 3. to conquer – 4. to reinforce – 5. evident – 6. ethnic – 7. affairs – 8. subject – 9. application – 10. disparity

e) 1. formerly – 2. independent – 3. to be part of – 4. to join – 5. application – 6. symbolic – 7. links – 8. equal – 9. encouragement – 10. human rights – 11. role – 12. exclusive – 13. to oppose – 14. cultural activities – 15. particularly

2.4 World of work

a)

Noun	Verb	Adjective
– application – Bewerbung, Anwendung	– to apply – sich bewerben, anwenden	– applicable – anwendbar
– recommendation – Empfehlung	– to recommend – empfehlen	– recommendable – empfehlenswert
– strength – Stärke	– to strengthen – stärken	– strong – stark

- acceleration - Beschleunigung	- to accelerate - beschleunigen	- - -
- equality - Gleichberechtigung	- to equalise - angleichen	- equal - gleich
- sufficiency - hinreichende Menge und Qualität	- to suffice - genügen	- sufficient - ausreichend
- doubt - Zweifel	- to doubt - zweifeln	- doubtful - zweifelhaft

b) 1. dull – 2. exploit – 3. to pursue – 4. to retire – 5. to urge – 6. to verify – 7. eager – 8. despite – 9. generous

c) 1. preparation – 2. key part – 3. commit – 4. impression – 5. properly – 6. employer – 7. achievements – 8. strengths – 9. state – 10. potential – 11. knowledge – 12. self-confidence – 13. beforehand – 14. position – 15. appearance – 16. interview – 17. make sure
(*proper* and *afterwards* don't fit.)

d) 1. are seeking – 2. to work – 3. must be – 4. have – 5. are required – 6. is – 7. Send
(*seek* and *is required* don't fit.)

2.5 Science, technology and society

a)

Noun	Verb	Adjective
- mutation, mutant - Mutation, Mutant	- to mutate - mutieren	- mutant - mutierend
- donation - Spende	- to donate - spenden	- - -
- cure - Heilmittel	- to cure - heilen	- curable, curative - heilbar, heilend
- inheritance, heritage - Erbe	- to inherit - erben	- hereditary - erblich
- resistance - Widerstand	- to resist - widerstehen	- resistant - widerstandsfähig

b) 1. fertility treatment – 2. yield – 3. tissue – 4. intruder – 5. to monitor – 6. surgery – 7. to clone – 8. power plant – 9. host – 10. hazardous

c) GM products

controversies

safety
- more **food allergies**
- GM plants could **breed** with natural plants (mutant superweeds)
- **unknown effect** on human health and other organisms

labelling
- not **mandatory** in some countries
- non-GM cropos are often **contaminated** with GM crops

society
- only rich countries might **benefit**

benefits

crops
- better resistance to disease and **pests**
- higher yields and **nutrients**
- **enhanced** taste and quality

environment
- fewer **poisonous** pesticides and herbicides
- **conservation** of soil, water and energy

society
- less starvation and **malnutrition**

2.6 The impact of change

a)

Noun	Verb	Adjective
– edition, editor – Ausgabe, Redakteur	– to edit – bearbeiten	– editorial – redaktionell
– innovation – Neuerung	– to innovate – Neuerungen vornehmen	– innovative – bahnbrechend
– regret – Bedauern	– to regret – bedauern	– regrettable – bedauerlich
– volunteer – Freiwillige/-r	– to volunteer – sich freiwillig melden	– voluntary – freiwillig
– value – Wert	– to value – bewerten	– valuable – wertvoll
– perishables (pl) – leicht verderbliche Waren	– to perish – verderben	– perishable – verderblich
– influence – Einfluss	– to influence – beeinflussen	– influential – einflussreich

b) 1. influential – 2. entertainment – 3. spends – 4. TV set – 5. state-run – 6. funded – 7. licence fees – 8. sponsored – 9. autonomy – 10. content – 11. private sector – 12. commercial breaks – 13. sponsor

c) 1. break – 2. press – 3. coverage – 4. material – 5. headline – 6. celebrities – 7. ad – 8. fee

d) 1. habit – 2. to pave the way – 3. reputation – 4. ingredient – 5. gist – 6. impact – 7. to rule – 8. poll – 9. retirement – 10. sensible

e) 1. reliance – 2. need – 3. groundbreaking – 4. storage – 5. gravy – 6. pace – 7. factual – 8. instant – 9. woeful – 10. edition – 11. innovation

2.7 Dreams and visions

a)

Noun	Verb	Adjective
- admiration - Bewunderung	- to admire - bewundern	- admirable - bewundernswert
- prosperity - Wohlstand	- to prosper - florieren, gedeihen	- prosperous - wohlhabend
- anxiety - Angst	– – –	- anxious - ängstlich
- residence - Wohnsitz	- to reside - seinen Sitz haben	- residential - Wohn-
- imagination - Vorstellung	- to imagine - sich vorstellen	- imaginary - erfunden

b) 1. remark, Bemerkung – 2. to appreciate, schätzen – 3. to conduct, ausführen – 4. invincible, unbesiegbar – 5. to draft, entwerfen – 6. to restore, wiederherstellen – 7. to recognise, anerkennen – 8. evident, offensichtlich – 9. fee, Gebühr – 10. loan, Kredit – 11. to retain, behalten

c) 1. merely – 2. nutrition – 3. revenue – 4. approval – 5. anxiety – 6. resistance – 7. fertilizer – 8. to trigger – 9. breakthrough – 10. barely – 11. solar energy

d) 1. soar – 2. medieval – 3. impartial – 4. fortnight – 5. predecessor – 6. amendment – 7. threat – 8. notion - 9. successor – 10. dissent – 11. admiration

2.8 Cross-cultural issues

a)

Noun	**Verb**	**Adjective**
- acceptance - Annahme	- to accept - annehmen	- acceptable - annehmbar
- offence/offender - Straftat, Beleidigung/ Straftäter(in)	- to offend - beleidigen	- offensive - beleidigend
- diversity - Vielfalt	- to diversify - diversifizieren	- diverse - mannigfaltig, verschieden
- promotion - Beförderung, Förderung	- to promote - fördern	- - -

b) 1. wear – 2. race relations – 3. remarks – 4. veil – 5. case – 6. teaching assistant – 7. language – 8. to take of – 9. refused – 10. suspended – 11. debate – 12. multi-culturalism – 13. customs – 14. terrorism – 15. doubts – 16. mainstream – 17. point out – 18. leaders – 19. tolerant – 20. stir

c) 1. mosque – 2. resident – 3. resentment – 4. custom – 5. fortunate – 6. victim – 7. hatred – 8. obey – 9. minority

d) Immigration

benefits for **society**
- **different food**
- new ideas and languages
- reduce the effects of an **ageing society** (often young and a lot of children)

benefits for the **economy**
- cheap **labour**
- innovative ideas and **entrepreneurial spirit**
- **business contacts** to other countries
- **skilled workers** in needed sectors

disadvantages for **society**
- often **scapegoats** for all kinds of problems
- racial **tensions**
- **discrimination** against **ethnic minorities**
- **lower wages** for unskilled workers

disadvantages for the **economy**
- often **inadequate** language skills
- almost no jobs for **unskilled immigrants**
- high **welfare expenses**

2.9 The global challenge

a) 1. relief – 2. cute 3. – aid – 4. threat – 5. inevitable – 6. asset – 7. to exacerbate – 8. foundation – 9. merger – 10. to incline – 11. subsidized – 12. precondition

b) 1. globalisation – 2. prosperity – 3. expects – 4. spread of freedom – 5. human rights – 6. conflicts – 7. opportunities – 8. understanding – 9. universal values – 10. stability – 11. fear – 12. foreign – 13. governments – 14. mass media – 15. predict – 16. immigration – 17. multinational companies – 18. governments – 19. humanity – 20. ethnic tensions – 21. pollution – 22. slogan – 23. gap

c)

Noun	Verb	Adjective
– response – Antwort	– to respond – reagieren	– responsive – ansprechbar, reagierend
– adaptability – Anpassungsfähigkeit	– to adapt – anpassen	– adaptable – anpassbar
– liberalisation – Freigabe	– to liberalise – liberalisieren	– liberal – liberal, frei
– prospect – Aussicht	– – –	– prospective – potenziell möglich
– globalisation – Globalisierung	– to globalise – globalisieren	– global – weltweit

d) 1. shares – 2. downturn – 3. blessing – 4. failure – 5. debt – 6. prospect – 7. to abolish – 8. to relocate – 9. approach – 10. sweatshop

e) Globalisation

company aspects

choosing best places for certain tasks
mobility of goods/capital/products
social responsibility of companies

preconditions
- **fast transportation worldwide**
- **information and communication technology**
- free trade

hopes
- **creation of new jobs**
- rising standard of living
- **new demand through innovation**

fears
- **companies make more and more profits**
- loss of work places
- **only the rich benefit**

2.10 Marketing, advertising and design

a)

Noun	**Verb**	**Adjective**
- exploitation - Ausbeutung	- to exploit - ausbeuten	- exploitative - ausbeuterisch
- sustainability - Nachhaltigkeit	- to sustain - etw. erhalten	- sustainable - nachhaltig
- desire - Begehren, Wunsch	- to desire - wünschen	- desirable - wünschenswert

b) 1. embarrassment – 2. to maintain – 3. proposal – 4. brand – 5. affiliation – 6. encouragement – 7. awkward – 8. poultry – 9. behaviour – 10. to tackle – 11. appeal – 12. to convince

c) 1. think – 2. tend – 3. shop – 4. matter – 5. buy – 6. summarizes – 7. are – 8. help – 9. go – 10. have to – 11. compare – 12. make – 13. feel – 14. think – 15. accomplished – 16. stay – 17. involves
(*pay* and *seen* don't fit)

d) 1. to mature – 2. exhibition – 3. bargain – 4. to coincide – 5. unique – 6. impact – 7. anxiety – 8. staff – 9. to struggle

e) 1. term – 2. happiness – 3. associated – 4. basic needs – 5. phenomenon – 6. widespread – 7. tendency – 8. identify – 9. status-enhancing – 10. shopaholics – 11. Opponents – 12. unnecessary – 13. display – 14. lacking
(*happy* and *necessary* don't fit)